WHOM He Raised

MELISSA SWONGER

Dedication

*To **Laura Casper**, whose radical kindness and persistent love, through the grace of the Father, became the catalyst for changing a legacy, and to her husband, **Bob Casper**, for creating space in their house and in his heart for us.*

*To **Darin**, for always believing my story was worth telling, always listening to them, and helping write them, for being willing to follow God when we don't understand, and for understanding the honor it is to be legacy changers.*

*To my girls, **Jessica, Sarah, Grace, and Gabriella "Ella,"** this...all of this...the hard work to heal, the commitment to keep going, the blueprint...ALL of this is for you and those who come after you. I am a legacy changer, but you all will change the world. Being your mom has been my greatest gift.*

*To "The Niece," **Crystalyn**, we understand what it is to have someone who comes, who stays, and who stands. I'm ridiculously grateful we've got to for each other, though I wish we could skip the stories that required it. You are and always have been a gift.*

Acknowledgments

To **Laura Casper**, who invested more than was rational; who saw worth in me that only God had seen before; who loved without limits; who came when I called—and when I didn't. You were a spiritual giant who taught me to sit at the feet of Jesus and fight on my knees. You mothered me, became a grandmother to my girls, and moved mountains in the process. You were the embodiment and living model of radical kindness—the kind that enables transformation and creates legacy changers. And to **Bob Casper**, who likely had no idea the spiritual battlefield he was stepping into when he came home from work and quietly straightened up our ADHD trail. Thank you for creating spaces that transform, for loving my family and me without question, and for seeing Laura the way I do—and more.

To my husband, **Darin**—at the time of this publication, we have just celebrated our 30th wedding anniversary. For all thirty of those years, I am fairly certain you believed this book, and so much more, was inside me waiting to come forth. Thank you for believing I am ten feet tall and bulletproof, especially during the seasons I did not believe that myself. Our family is my favorite part of this life.

To the world changers who are my daughters—**Jessica, Sarah, Grace, and Ella**—thank you for allowing all the unhealed versions of me along the way during the transformation process to be your mom. I am so grateful God chose me for the job. You inspire me daily. **Jessica**, the attorney who stands up to injustice and believes in change. **Sarah**, the physical therapist who overcame her own physical challenges and now helps others heal. **Grace**, whose extraordinary emotional intelligence allows her to sit with patients in critical moments—to rejoice and to weep with them. And **Ella**, who rounded out the tribe—the curious one who absorbs science like a sponge and will choose to use her gifts to heal and restore.

These brilliant women shine like diamonds in a world that often forgets what kindness looks like.

And to the OG member of the Tribe, **Crystalyn**—you carried the torch and lit the way. You lead the Avengers in the pursuit of justice, but let's not forget to have fun along the way. Keep taking one step forward for one more day. **Ransom, Anderson, Elijah, and Jensen** are gifts in this world, and they are also beyond blessed to have you as their treasure.

To **Erica Elliott**, you have listened to *all* the stories over the years and knew there was not just a book—but several—waiting to be written. Thank you for your love, friendship, encouragement, and prayers, and for being my business adventurer along the way.

To **Hanna Olivas**, thank you for taking a chance on me and my stories, even while being vulnerable with your own. Thank you for modeling grace in the midst of chaos and for holding space for both business and friendship. Because of that, we get to do this life together—with support, collaboration, and without compartmentalization. To the rest of the **Fab 6—Sonya, my long-distance bestie; Amie; and Yuliana**—you made this launch a joy. You reminded me what it means to pursue passion and to find joy along the way.

To **Dr. Rodney Cooper**, my advisor and professor at Gordon-Conwell Theological Seminary—thank you for telling me to write my story, even if it took six years to listen to the directive, and for believing in me during small beginnings. You challenged me to become the best version of who God intended me to be. And to **Dr. Jay Colker**, my dissertation chair and professor at Adler University—thank you for your patience, your belief, and most of all, your kindness.

Foreword
by Robert E. "Bob" Casper

I'll never forget that moment. The doorbell rang, and there stood Melissa with Jessica, Sarah, Grace, and Ella, all five of them exhausted but beaming after driving straight through from Arkansas. Twenty-plus hours on the road, and they'd made it. It was April 17, 2020.

Just hours earlier, my son Joe and I had brought my wife, Laura, home from the Cleveland Clinic in Vero Beach, Florida.

At only sixty-nine years old, Laura's life was slipping away under the relentless weight of heart disease and Parkinson's. Yet when she saw Melissa and the girls she loved so dearly, something remarkable happened. Laura's eyes lit up. Her spirit lifted. Love filled the room. Melissa and her daughters remained with her until the end, late into the night on April 17th– holding hands, hugging, crying, smiling, singing, praying, and praising God together.

That final, urgent journey was so characteristic of the Melissa I have always known: courageous, driven, and grounded in faith and love. She dropped everything to be present, to bear witness, and to walk alongside those she loved. That same spirit flows through every page of her book, *Whom He Raised*.

In her book, Melissa invites us into her life through three movements: The Grave, The Calling, and The Witness. Each reveals how God works not only in moments of strength, but also in stillness, surrender, and waiting.

As I read, I was struck by a realization I already sensed to be true: Laura had been part of a holy catalyst in Melissa's journey. Melissa writes, *"She (Laura) showed me that silence had been costly. However, there was an alternative way to move forward. Transformation was possible, and I could be transformed by the renewing of my mind (Romans 12:2). Radical kindness was the catalyst – the spark that lit the flame to ignite sustainable change."*

What makes this book extraordinary isn't just Melissa's story. It's what she's done with it. At the intersection of her experiences, her deep faith, and her rigorous education in psychology and theology, she's discovered something many people desperately need: a framework for transformation that actually works.

The blueprint that emerges from these pages is not theory, but hard-won wisdom gained through real suffering and healing. Melissa demonstrates that radical kindness is not weakness, but a powerful catalyst for change.

I believe Melissa's core message is this: Transformation does not happen through force, urgency, or pressure. It happens through radical kindness that creates safety for truth to emerge. Melissa discovered that the same conditions that brought healing to her could also heal others.

This is not a book you will read quickly. Melissa writes with patience and purpose. She does not rush the reader toward resolution and bypass the parts that hurt. Instead, she lays out the complexities, trusts you to handle the weight, and invites you to follow her personal journey.

Whom He Raised is ultimately about hope. No matter how deep the grave or how long the darkness is, transformation is possible. Not through our own strength, but through surrender to a God whose kindness never fails and whose calling in our lives is unstoppable.

—Robert E. (Bob) Casper

Foreword
by Darin Swonger

As Melissa's husband, I've had the front-row seat to her extraordinary journey—some of these points hit too close to home, if you know what I mean, stirring memories that still bring tears to my eyes. From the heart-wrenching depths of grief and betrayal to a profound, soul-stirring resurrection through unshakeable faith and renewed purpose. In Whom He Raised, she pours out this story with raw, vulnerable honesty, weaving her psychological expertise with spiritual truths that have not only transformed our lives but healed my own wounded heart.

I've watched her rise with awe and overwhelming pride—not just survive the storm, but thrive with a fierce, radiant light as Founder of The Sage Hill Project, guiding others toward deep healing and radical kindness that touches the soul. This book isn't just her memoir; it's a powerful testament to God's irrevocable calling (Romans 11:29), a beacon of hope and a heartfelt guide for anyone craving renewal amid their own pain.

I'm immensely proud of Melissa—my love, my partner, my inspiration—and I know her words will stir your spirit, lifting you higher than you ever imagined.

—Darin Swonger

Foreword
by Hanna Olivas

Some books are written because the author has something to say.

This book exists because something sacred had to be told.

Whom He Raised is not a story you consume. It is a story you enter. And once you do, you don't leave unchanged.

I have had the honor of walking alongside Melissa Swonger not just as her publisher, but as a witness to the woman behind these pages, the one who didn't rush her healing, didn't package her pain, and didn't turn her story into something tidy or marketable. She chose truth over polish. Depth over speed. Obedience over comfort. And that choice is felt in every chapter of this book.

This is not a resurrection story in the way we often expect them. It doesn't begin with triumph. It begins in the grave. In the places most people work desperately to avoid naming. In the slow accumulation of trauma, silence, endurance, and survival that so many learn to call strength. Melissa does not sensationalize these places, nor does she minimize them. She honors them by telling the truth about what it costs to live there, and what it takes to be called out.

What struck me most as I read was not just what Melissa survived, but how she paid attention. Attention to the body. Attention to the nervous system. Attention to God when productivity and urgency were stripped away. This book is deeply informed by her education and experience in psychology and theology, but it is never academic. It is embodied. It is lived. It is practiced wisdom, earned through suffering and refined through surrender.

Melissa writes with a rare integrity, one that refuses to weaponize faith or rush the reader toward resolution. She understands that healing is not linear, that obedience often looks like stillness, and that radical kindness is not weakness but the very condition that makes transformation possible. This is not a book about fixing yourself. It is a book about finally feeling safe enough to tell the truth and discovering that God meets us there.

As the founder of She Rises Studios, I have had the privilege of holding space for many powerful stories. But some stories change the room when they are spoken. Whom He Raised is one of them. It invites us to reconsider what it means to be strong, faithful, and alive. It challenges the lie that survival is the same as living, and it gently, but firmly calls us to something more.

If you are reading this book, I believe it is not by accident. Perhaps you, too, have learned how to endure. Perhaps you have stood for so long that sitting feels unsafe. Perhaps you have mistaken vigilance for wisdom, urgency for obedience, or silence for strength. This book is an invitation, not to perform your healing, but to receive it.

Melissa's story reminds us that being raised does not always look like rising up. Sometimes it looks like staying still long enough to hear your name spoken in a place you once believed only held loss.

May you read these pages with courage.

May you allow yourself to be interrupted.

And may you discover that the same God who raised her is still calling forth life quietly, kindly, relentlessly in you.

With deep respect and gratitude,
Hanna Olivas
Founder & CEO, She Rises Studios Publishing

Table of Contents

Introduction

I did not set out to write a story about being raised, well, I didn't set out to write *my* story at all.

I wrote because I was interrupted.

Again.

There are moments in life when interruption feels like sabotage—when the floor gives way beneath your feet and the familiar strategies you rely on no longer work. I have lived through enough of those moments to recognize the pattern. Injury. Loss. Disorientation. The quiet dismantling of who I thought I needed to be in order to survive.

And that's just physical disruption. There are moments in life that take your breath away. When you forget how to breathe and are disoriented. When the world should stop for a moment to acknowledge the trauma and just let you catch your breath, but instead keeps spinning and moving in a way that no longer involves you.

Then, eventually, you have to figure out how to merge back into life after trauma. Or, don't. Sometimes we put on a mask and behave in ways the world assumes we have reassimilated. But the truth lies hidden within hypervigilance, in standing, and silence that are paltry counterfeits to rest and stillness.

For a long time, I believed those interruptions were obstacles to the life I was meant to live—detours from a story that would make more sense if it could just unfold uninterrupted.

I was wrong.

This book was written from a place I did not expect to return to: a state of stillness. Not the kind of stillness you schedule or curate, but the kind that arrives when motion is no longer available and productivity loses its power to distract. The kind that exposes what is left when endurance is no longer enough.

It was there—flat on my back, stripped of urgency—that I finally asked the question I had been avoiding:

What would you like me to do with this?

Rather than an answer, relief, or explanation, it did not arrive as instruction or reassurance; it offered orientation.

This story unfolds in three movements.

The Grave is not a metaphor. It is the environment formed by repeated threats, loss, and adaptation—the place where survival becomes a skill and silence becomes a strategy. It is where endurance is learned, vigilance is rewarded, and standing becomes reflex. This is the internal place of trauma. Many of us live there longer than we realize, mistaking survival for strength and function for freedom.

The Calling is not a job description or a spiritual promotion. It is the slow dismantling of survival identities that once worked and no longer fit. It is the courage to listen when urgency loses authority, to remain present when clarity does not arrive on demand, and to question whether responsibility has become the only way we know how to be faithful. It has a dual meaning: being called forth from the darkness and as our Calling for all that comes next.

The Witness is not performance. It is not platform. It is not proof. It is what happens when formation bears fruit quietly—when a life lived in alignment begins to create space for others without needing to explain itself.

This is not a book about triumph.

It is a book about integration.

It is written for those who have survived long enough to realize that survival is not the same as living, and is a far cry from thriving. For those who learned to stand because standing was necessary and part of being watchful—and are now being invited to sit, listen, and reorient. For those who are tired of urgency masquerading as obedience, productivity disguising itself as purpose, and faith that only works when things are moving forward.

I do not offer answers here.

I offer attention and intention.

Attention to the places where silence and vigilance have been confused with wisdom. Attention to the ways our bodies remember what our minds try to outgrow. Attention to the quiet invitations that arrive not when life is finally under control, but when control is no longer available.

Because sometimes being raised does not look like rising up.

Sometimes it looks like staying still long enough to hear your name spoken in a place you once believed only held loss.

And sometimes, that is where the story truly begins.

The Grave

"Lord, [s]he whom You love is sick.' When Jesus heard this, He said, 'This sickness will not end in death; but [on the contrary it is] for the glory *and* honor of God, so that the Son of God may be glorified by it."
— (John 12:4, AMP)

CHAPTER 1

The Trap Door

"Out of the depths, I cry to You, Lord."
— (Psalms 130:1)

Long before I fell through the trap door, something in me had already begun to descend.

I didn't know how to name it then. I only knew the feeling—the quiet tightening in my chest, the way my body braced even when nothing appeared wrong, the sense that life required vigilance even in moments of rest. I had learned early how to survive. How to stay alert. How to keep moving when stopping felt unsafe.

So when the trap door opened beneath my feet, the shock was immediate—but the recognition was deeper.

Six months ago, I fell through a trap door.

Not figuratively. Literally.

The concrete and metal swallowed me. The sound of my body hitting the bottom echoed through the small space, sharp and final. Then came the silence. A silence so complete it felt heavier than the fall itself. I remember lying there, stunned, thinking, *So this is how it happens.* And then—strangely—I laughed. Just once. A short, half-hearted sound that surprised me.

Adrenaline has a way of letting physical pain arrive last.

Real-life trap doors don't come with cinematic recoveries. They come with stillness. With the realization that your body is no longer cooperating. With the dawning awareness that you are no longer in control.

Above me, I heard movement—my daughter screaming my name, footsteps growing urgent. Her voice was a desperate plea for me to be alright. Her brain knew what her eyes were seeing wasn't an illusion. She would later say she wanted to run away from the sight of me in that tomb. Ha. Me too!

But the will to stay when others run courses through her veins. She begged me to call an ambulance. I told her to call her father. His deep, calm voice, trained through years of leading actual life-or-death emergencies, spoke through her panic. He asked her to put her clinical brain in gear, climb into the pit with me, and give the assessment. Her leg shook so badly behind my back, I thought there was a slithering snake down with us.

"Take the ambulance," they said. "Now."

I refused.

Not because I was fine. Not because I was brave. Not because I didn't understand the severity. But because something older than logic was already dictating my choices. Not knowing the extent of my injuries and with sheer determination, I army-crawled my way out, my daughter holding my leg in extension, my body acting long before my mind could catch up.

I didn't analyze that choice at the time. I didn't need to. My nervous system already knew what to do: stay quiet, get out, don't draw attention.

Trauma doesn't ask permission. It defaults to what it learned long ago.

Once I was out, the world felt louder. Brighter. Exposed. The garage—my own garage—suddenly felt like a public place. I wanted to get inside without anyone seeing, without the neighborhood noticing, without the uninvited spectacle of needing help. But I couldn't sit up or even roll over. Somehow, using stacked coolers and adrenaline, I climbed into my Jeep Wrangler face down at an angle and, with fingers gripping the sides, nose pressed into the door, belying the soothing voice with which I asked my daughter to take a deep breath and remain calm as she drove me to the hospital.

It is amazing what the body prioritizes in a crisis: not comfort, not safety, not even wisdom—but *control.* Or the illusion of it.

By the time I reached the bed, the truth had settled in.

No weight bearing. No sitting. No crutches because of the fractured spine in two places. And the avulsion fracture in my pelvis. Torn hamstring muscles had bled into my thigh, hip, and groin, leaving ghastly swelling and bruising. Even lying down wasn't a relief—it was endurance.

And hanging in the air was a familiar word.

Again.

That word didn't just describe injury. It described a pattern.

It described the way life had interrupted me before. Suffering has been a recurring theme in my story. The way I have learned to rebuild a life from the ground up and then, just as I began to stand steady, felt the ground shift again beneath me–again.

People have called my life an Old Testament "Job-like" existence. I understand why. The timeline reads like an erratic EKG with peaks and plunges, breakthroughs and collapses, laughter and grief stitched together in ways that don't always make sense on paper. Epigenetic trauma. Medical trauma. Dysfunction. Abuse. Loss. Betrayal. Recovery. Repeat.

I can tell you the clinical language for what constant unpredictability does to a human nervous system. I can name the hypervigilance. The overthinking. The way the body learns to scan for danger even in safe places. I can explain Complex PTSD and the brain's tendency to keep old footage on replay as a sort of training manual lest we forget what trauma has forged.

But what matters more than the terminology is the lived experience: There are people who walk through life expecting good. And there are people who walk through life waiting for the other shoe to fall. That waiting becomes a kind of grave.

The fall through the trap door happened after I returned from one of those seasons that change your DNA. I had celebrated my daughter's graduation from law school—one of the proudest moments of motherhood—on the heels of walking through the horrific loss of my two-and-a-half-year-old great-nephew with my niece and her family. I'd moved in with them for the greater part of the last ten months to love on his mama, their family, and rock a dying baby. I stayed six weeks after he passed, then we all went to celebrate my oldest daughter's graduation from law school out east. Though unbidden, grief came too, refusing to stay politely in its own chapter. It bleeds into everything.

I came home carrying both joy and devastation, trying to merge back into life after trauma. I had plans. Goals. A strategy. The coach and psychologist in me were hard at work building the roadmap.

Just as I was trying to stand once more, before I could even get inside the house, the storm shelter in the garage floor opened and took me down.

As I lay in bed, unable to move, I skipped over denial. I skipped over anger. I even skipped over disappointment faster than I expected. Not because those feelings weren't available to me, but because I had been here before. Bed rest with miscarriages. Bed rest with births. Bed rest with recovery from another freak accident that had left me in a wheelchair, relearning how to walk for four years. Illnesses threatening to take my life, or make me wish it would. The bed is familiar territory for someone whose body has repeatedly demanded surrender.

But the trap door was different.

It wasn't just an injury; it was a catalyst for a different type of surrender that resolved delayed obedience, a divine interruption. It was the stripping away of the ability to distract myself with productivity. The removal of my usual coping mechanisms. The forced confrontation with stillness.

And it was in that stillness that I found myself sitting with God in a way I hadn't in a long time, not as the high-functioning woman who knows the right verses and can hold everyone else together, but as a person who was flat on her back, exposed, and finally out of options.

Yes, I know that in this world, we will face tribulation. Jesus promised as much (John 16:33). But when tribulation keeps returning—when the *again* begins to stack—it can start to feel less like a season and more like a sentence.

So this time, I became all ears.

This time, I didn't default to the old, well-worn pathways of victimhood, self-protection, or numbing. I simply asked the most honest question I had: *"What would You like me to do with this?"*

And that question became a turning point. Not because pain instantly transformed into purpose, but because something in me finally stopped fighting reality long enough to receive instruction.

What I found was another miracle: the chance to begin again.

Not the kind of "begin again" that comes with a clean slate and a fresh calendar. The kind that comes with bruises and immobility, with limits and dependence, with the humbling truth that you cannot muscle your way through everything. The kind of beginning that requires surrender.

I thought about the Israelites in the wilderness—forty years for an eleven-day trek. Circling the same mountain, again and again, as God tried to lead their fearful, disoriented hearts into freedom. It wasn't the distance that took them so long. It was the transformation.

And there I was, flat on my back, wondering if the *again* in my story was not God's cruelty—but God's pursuit.

While He had my undivided attention—and the first thing I did as soon as I could sit up at an incline enough to use my computer and with zero other distractions because I was incapable of doing anything else—I began to write. Not because I felt inspired, but because I felt called.

I began writing down my conversation with God and grasping His vision, which we could already guess was bigger than mine and far outside my comfort zone.

The life verse He gave me long ago demanded I look at myself in the grave, heed my calling, and serve as a witness: "...and they came, not only because of Jesus, but also to see [*Melissa*], whom He raised from the dead" (John 12:9b).

I let Him come to the places that had been dead for too long. I let Him call me forth by name. And for the first time, I stopped seeing my story as a series of interruptions and began to see it as an invitation: to move from survival to life, from functioning to freedom, from hiding to witness.

This book is told in three sections.

The Grave is the story of the trauma that put me in the tomb—some visible, some invisible, all formative.

The Calling is the courage to take one step forward out of darkness when I don't yet know what healing will require, but do so because I believe there is something more to receive, and a willingness to pour from what I have. It has a dual meaning here: being called forth out of the grave and receiving my Calling for my life's direction.

The Witness is where I stand now—at the intersection of my personal experience, my faith, and the education God led me to pursue, which creates space for others to transform.

Join me on a journey through trials, triumphs, and heartbreaks to the truth of a new beginning. The lessons I learned in the process apply to all of us and show us how to receive an abundant life this side of Heaven (John 10:10), with beauty for our ashes (Isaiah 61:3), because He is doing a new thing (Isaiah 43:19).

But first, we have to tell the truth about the grave.

Because resurrection is not a metaphor for the person who has been buried alive.

And for me, it began with a trap door.

"See, I am doing a new thing! Now it springs up; do you not perceive it? I am making a way in the wilderness and streams in the wasteland." — (Isaiah 43:19)

But Did You Die?

"Even though I walk through the [sunless] valley of the shadow of death, I fear no evil, for You are with me."
— Psalm 23:4a (AMP)

But did you die?

It sounds flippant written out like that. Almost dismissive. But in our family, it wasn't sarcasm, it was shorthand. A way of naming the thin line between danger and survival. A way of laughing in the face of fear so fear didn't get the final word.

But did you die? meant:
You're shaken, but you're here.
You're scared, but you're breathing.
You survived, so keep moving.

In a family shaped by neurodivergent ADHD brains (often mistaken for anxiety in girls), trauma-fueled epigenetic lines, and a long history of bracing rather than resting, fear had a way of slipping quietly into the driver's seat if we weren't paying attention. Not loud fear. Not panic. The subtle kind. The kind that disguises itself as caution and masquerades as wisdom but is a counterfeit whose result is regret and catastrophizing.

So we made a rule: We don't make fear-based decisions.

Fear is deeply personal. One person's *Absolutely not* is another person's *Let's go.* With four daughters, meeting each one where she was meant to be courageous would look different for each of them. For one, it meant standing on a stage. For another, it meant confronting speed, height, or anything that made her stomach drop before her feet left the ground.

Our youngest embraced the motto with particular enthusiasm. She didn't flirt with danger recklessly, but she refused to let fear narrate her life. She looked risk in the eye and dared it to make a move, which left her parents with one eye always watching and calculating in an attempt to predict her next move.

That posture—half bravery, half defiance—felt familiar to me. It mirrored something I had learned long before I had words for it: if you can laugh at danger, you don't have to feel how close it came. It is also a requisite to slay bullies.

That belief would be put to the test one afternoon in California.

We were there for soccer, as usual. Most of our family vacations were planned around national youth tournaments, with a few "fun days" tacked on so we could pretend we were spontaneous people instead of logistical experts navigating team hotels, recruitment strategies, and bracket schedules.

One of those days involved renting electric scooter-style bikes—no pedals—to ride from San Diego over to Coronado Island.

We weren't familiar with the area. You were technically supposed to be sixteen with a driver's license to use the bikes. Our youngest was fifteen without even a driver's permit, which we pointed out matter-of-factly. The rental place waved it off with a smile and a shrug.

"It's just like riding a bike."

Less than a mile in, she lost control.

It happened fast—too fast for adrenaline to fully engage. She clipped a curb in traffic while trying to slow for a red light and nearly flipped over the handlebars. For a suspended second, everything froze. And then—somehow—she recovered.

We all stopped. Hearts pounding. Hands shaking.

She was upright. Breathing. Alive.

And after the moment passed, we did what our family had learned to do.

We kept going.

The traffic didn't improve. To reach the ferry port, we had to cross ten lanes of traffic and ride in front of the airport—yes, the airport—like we were locals who did this every weekend. Darin took the lead. Two of our daughters followed him. I brought up the rear.

The ride was intense, but the day was worth it. We explored the island with the wind in our faces and enjoyed its historic sites. When it came time to head back, we felt like we'd mastered it. The only hiccup was the GPS device that came loose from the bike in the parking lot before boarding the ferry, leaving us a bit blind in the areas around the port where cell service was unreliable. All was set to end the excursion on a high note.

Then we got separated.

No GPS. Different bike speeds. An on-ramp that appeared to lead to the highway but was actually a road we could have navigated. Darin disappeared ahead of us on that road, unable to hear us calling, unable to see us under the overpass.

There we were, under a highway, in a strange city, on motorized bikes we probably shouldn't have been on, relying on instinct and prayer and the faint sense that guardian angels were clocking overtime.

There was nothing to do but laugh.

And walk with the God of Angel Armies.

Eventually, we found a sketchy gas station that looked like it had seen better decades…or maybe not. The attendant looked at us like we had lost our minds—which, to be fair, might have been accurate—and pointed us in the right direction. In fact, all of the people around the gas station and under the overpass gave us the same incredulous look. We crested a hill, regained cell service, called Darin, and found our way back to each other and then to the bike rental return.

We took pictures that day. The kind that flattens reality into smiles and sunshine. The kind that don't show the moments where a slightly different outcome would have turned that story into something else entirely.

Later, over tacos, someone finally asked the question.

But did you die?

No.

We laughed. We always did.

But that question—harmless on the surface—was doing more work than we realized.

Because there are stories where, *but did you die?* is a punchline.

And there are stories where it becomes a worldview.

I was born about eight weeks early in 1973. My lungs were underdeveloped and never really learned to breathe well. Childhood, for me, included near misses with breathing, asthma attacks, and rushed trips to hospitals. I missed months of school at a time and learned early that air was not guaranteed.

Survival wasn't theoretical. It was physiological.

When I was fifteen, I had suffered from a sinus infection for five years that refused to resolve. A CT scan revealed I was missing protective eye bones and had deformed sinuses that weren't allowing proper ventilation or drainage. The ENT was stunned that my face hadn't collapsed on one side. The fix was surgery.

An incision inside my mouth where my upper gums meet my cheek. My face lifted. Holes were drilled into my skull to facilitate drainage. The surgeon was honest: given my facial structure, a millimeter error could render me blind.

I remember what I wore that morning. You were supposed to wear "good clothes," I suppose, maybe in case this was your last moment on earth. It certainly wasn't for the staff, who would only see me in a hospital gown. Still, I had a perfect French braid. This fifteen-year-old did not want an OR hairnet ruining her hair.

I was scared. No one but my mother knew just how much, because it was by her design.

The surgery appeared to go as planned.

Until it didn't.

After extubation, I quit breathing.

Though I was mostly out of it, I remember the pain of shock—violent shaking—just before alarms erupted. Lights flashed. People ran. The room filled with a flurry of split-second decisions while I felt desperately out of control.

And then...*peace*.

Not numbness. Not darkness. Not worry or chaos.

Peace.

No pain. No fear. No urgency. Just peace as I hovered over my bed, watching what was happening...*to me.*

Near-death experiences vary, but for me, the defining feature was not spectacle. It was a choice. I knew I could stay. I also knew I could go back.

Jesus was there. Not frantic. Not distressed. Completely at peace with the storm below—which was my body. This reality that the person dying isn't experiencing the pain of death as we interpret it, because the person dying is suspended from feeling before taking their final breath, has brought comfort to loved ones at the bedside more than once.

I did not want to leave that peace.

But I also knew, with a clarity that bypassed logic, that my time was not finished. I had work to do on earth that I could not yet name.

So I yielded.

I went back.

The return to my body was violent. Pain rushed in. Chaos followed. I forced my eyes open and focused on the clock across the room, too blurry to read. I believed that if I could just bring it into focus, I could fight my way back into my body. And, regain control.

Half my face was packed and bandaged. Because of earlier trauma—so many moments of not being able to breathe—I had developed a fear of masks strapped to my face. I needed control. I prefer to hold the masks myself. Or, allow them to prop it lightly near my nose and mouth.

My chart read in bold print: Do not strap masks to her face.

Most thought I had been through enough for one day. But compassion wasn't a strength of my PACU nurse. She ignored it, strapping the mask to my face. Though not in charge of my faculties, panic rose from a depth I had no energy to quell.

I swiped at the mask. She scolded me. Strapped it on again. The third time, with strength I didn't know I had, and an accuracy that could only be attributed to a remaining gust of the Holy Spirit, I kicked her in her stomach and sent her across the room. It was a panicked flail, but it hit the mark.

She slid.

To be fair, she had been warned. I got a new nurse.

I ended up in the ICU next to a college student who had been in a coma after a car-versus-train accident. She woke up shortly after I arrived. The lone survivor.

I guess it wasn't her time either.

That day, my body didn't die. But something else did. Trust. Innocence. The belief that adults always tell the truth, that people who promise or are tasked with caring for you will, and that betrayal is a soul-deep sucking chest wound.

In the weeks leading up to surgery, my mother had convinced me I had brain cancer. She said that doctors were hiding it from me so I wouldn't worry. She told me my face would be disfigured. That holes would be drilled through my face and would never close or may scar over, but their proof would always remain.

When I asked for a mirror post-op, she refused, telling the nurses not to bring one so as not to upset me. Finally, desperate, I begged. A nurse brought the surgeon. They held up the mirror. I was swollen. Bruised. One side of my smile was paralyzed by the severed nerves until they could reroute themselves over the next few months.

But there were no holes.

None.

My mother laughed it off. "It was a joke," she said. "We didn't think you'd really believe that."

Something in me shut down. Love died that day. And seeds of unforgiveness, full of bitterness, took root.

I lived. But I learned something dangerous.

That as long as you survive, you're fine.
That fear is manageable if you keep moving.
The goal is not wholeness, but endurance.

But did you die?

No.

But parts of me learned how to live in the shadow of death, and that shadow would follow me into every grave others dug for me, and even ones I had dug myself.

"O Lord my God, I cried to You for help, and You have healed me. O Lord, You have brought my life up from Sheol, the place of the dead; You have kept me alive, so that I would not go down to the pit." — Psalm 30:2–3 (AMP)

CHAPTER 3

Death by a Thousand Cuts

"He heals the brokenhearted and binds up their wounds [healing their pain and comforting their sorrow]." — Psalm 147:3 (AMP)

Some wounds appear stealthily, like the bruises you can't quite remember getting.

They don't arrive with sirens or blood or a single moment you can point to and say, *That's when everything changed.* Instead, they come quietly. Incrementally. One small cut at a time. And because none of them seem catastrophic on their own, you learn to minimize them. To normalize them. To move on. However, the cumulative quality of them together rewire a brain from connection to protection, never knowing when another blow will strike.

Fear did not arrive all at once.

It came in fragments—small enough to be absorbed without protest, frequent enough to become familiar. I did not experience it as panic. I experienced it as readiness. A quiet hum beneath everything, alerting me to the fact that something could change without warning.

My body learned before my mind did.

I learned how to listen for shifts in tone. How to read rooms the way other children read books. I could tell when laughter meant safety and when it meant danger. I learned the difference between footsteps that passed by and footsteps that stopped.

No one told me to do this. There were no instructions. It was simply what kept me from being surprised.

Surprise felt dangerous. So I eliminated it where I could.

Even in moments that looked ordinary—sitting at the table, lying in bed, playing quietly—I was tracking variables. Who was home? Who wasn't? How long had it been since something went wrong? Whether the atmosphere felt brittle or forgiving.

This vigilance did not feel heroic. It felt responsible.

I didn't yet know that responsibility taken too early becomes a burden, or that vigilance practiced too long becomes exhaustion. All I knew was that being prepared felt safer than being caught off guard.

That kind of damage is harder to name.

It's easier to talk about falling through a trap door than it is to talk about the slow erosion of safety. It's easier to explain a surgery than it is to explain what it feels like to grow up never fully relaxed, never certain the ground beneath you will hold.

By the time I was old enough to understand the word *trauma*, my body already knew it by heart.

I learned early how to read a room. How to listen for footsteps. How to detect mood shifts before words are spoken. I learned that calm could shatter without warning, and that when it did, the safest place to be was invisible.

No one sat me down and taught me this. It was absorbed, the way children absorb gravity.

My childhood was shaped by illness as much as environment. I was born about eight weeks early. My lungs never quite caught up. Breathing—something most people never think about—was not a guarantee for me. Asthma attacks. Hospital runs. Near misses. The kind of moments where adults rush and speak in clipped tones, while you focus on the effort of getting air into your body, and you use your arms to sit more upright to help your lungs receive air. The air we take for granted betrayed my body as even enough air to utter the word *Help!* could not be found.

I missed months of school at a time.

Hospitals became familiar. Not comforting—just familiar. They smelled like antiseptic and fear. Doctors and nurses tried to be kind, but kindness doesn't always translate to safety when your body is already in a state of panic. After the medical storm, the staff and even my family usually thought candy or another treat would help. As if sugar could overwrite terror.

Illness complicated everything. My body did not feel like a neutral, or even collaborative, partner. Breathing was something I thought about—something I managed, measured, and monitored. Medications altered my appearance and my energy. Hospital rooms reeked of valiant attempts to sanitize loss and cover over raw emotions. This is where I learned to read adults' faces the way we read weather patterns.

Concern looked different depending on who wore it.

I learned early that my body could betray me without warning. That weakness was not optional. That control was something you reached for because the alternative was chaos. At home, illness did not grant protection. At school, it marked me. In public, it invited commentary. I learned how to minimize symptoms, how to downplay pain, and how to present functionality even when my body was asking for rest.

Being sick did not excuse me from expectation. It intensified it. So I learned to keep going. I learned to endure. Endurance became my strength and my hiding place.

At home, the atmosphere was unpredictable. My father worked long hours and was rarely present. He wasn't generally physically or verbally abusive, but he also refused to temper my mother, who was. When he was around, she restrained herself. When he wasn't, the house felt different.

I don't know how much he truly knew. I only know his refrain: *I'll have to live with her long after you're gone* was well-known to his children.

Even as a child, I understood that meant my safety was negotiable.

There were six of us, but it often felt like two separate families. The older three and the younger three. I was the youngest. My oldest brother, fifteen years older, played the role of buffer and comic relief. He knew how to make things lighter. How to distract our mother. How to turn a moment into laughter.

He made "bathtub Kool-Aid" when the dishwasher was running (because the old dishwashers had to be connected to the kitchen faucet by a hose), complete with a song and dance that transformed the ordinary into magic. He put football helmets on my head and declared my missed kicks "gooood!" with theatrical enthusiasm. He spun me like an airplane when I "won."

And then he left. He went into the military when I was three.

And that was that.

The house felt different after that. Quieter. Heavier. Less protected.

My oldest sister left for nursing school when I was two years old, a year before my brother left. I have one memory of her babysitting me—

singing "One Tin Soldier" while I cried. Music has a way of becoming deeply embedded in the body. I can still feel the cadence of that song when I think of her.

We weren't close after she left, if we ever were at all. I was only a toddler. She moved. Life moved on. Distance grew. And eventually, we moved too, settling in the Kansas City area when I was four years old.

The house in Kansas City had a double backyard, half basketball court, where I learned to roller skate. It also featured a playhouse with real glass windows and a shingled roof. It never quite regained the glory I had imagined it deserved. My favorite part was that my bedroom was pink, with pink-and-white shag carpet, and I thought it was the best thing in the world, especially a haven where I sought safety.

Though I was young and couldn't articulate the feeling, I now know that for a moment, it felt like a fresh start.

However, changing geography can't make you happy, especially when we don't address what isn't healed that requires a fresh start to begin with.

The unresolved baggage moved with us. By the time I was four years old, that meant a family culture deeply steeped in its own trauma and that of all those who came before us. I think my parents would have liked to break off the family curses and change the legacy themselves, and in some ways, they began the process. They were better parents than their own. What kind of home life makes a twelve-year-old girl (my mother) marry a twenty-two-year-old college football player (my father)? Whatever horrors lived there, I remind myself as I recount my own childhood, and especially now as I stand at the intersection of my personal experience, my faith, and my education, I know she simply didn't have the tools or the capacity to get there on her own.

After my brother left and we moved to Kansas City, my ten-year-older sister became my protector. She stood up to my mother in ways no one else did. That courage came at a cost. Their fights were explosive. Loud. Physical. I remember sitting on the stairs with my brother, two years older than me, watching a particularly violent episode unfold.

And then she was gone.

The day my sister left is a defining moment in my story.

There was screaming. Chaos. Accusations. And then silence. The god-awful silence signifies that the storm has ended, but new pain takes hold as the devastation is assessed, and the damage is massive. It's like when a natural disaster hits and the survivors who remain stare in stunned silence as they recognize their lives will never be the same, but they keep going because the world refuses to stop spinning to let them catch their breath.

I was not allowed to say goodbye.

I was barred from her room while she packed, as my mother physically barricaded the door, and I cried trying to break through to my sister, who was also sobbing. I couldn't hug her. Couldn't speak to her. Couldn't ask where she was going or when I would see her again. I watched her walk out, and she looked into my teary eyes with a clarity and a rage that pierced straight through me.

"Don't ever let her hit you," she said. "Do not let anyone ever hit you again."

And I didn't. The words were etched in stone in my little brain, maybe even into my soul. It became the only boundary I knew at such an early age.

But what no one tells you is that when the calm after the storm hits abruptly without repair, the aftermath can be just as damaging. There was no grief counseling. No acknowledgment. No apology. No processing. We were expected to move on as if nothing had happened.

But something *had* happened. Being asked to go on as if it didn't is one of the worst forms of gaslighting. Silence settled in like dust.

And what is kept in silence grows.

Night became the worst time. Falling asleep was difficult. Staying asleep was worse. Every sound felt threatening. Every creak carried possibility. My body never fully powered down. I was afraid of everything, though I couldn't always articulate exactly what *it* was.

Night was where fear was practiced.

Daylight offered distraction. Noise. Structure. People moving around. Night stripped all of that away. Sounds traveled farther. Silence stretched thinner. My body never fully powered down.

I lay in bed listening—not casually, but deliberately. I listened for doors opening and closing. For voices muffled by walls. For the absence of sound, which could mean peace or could mean something gathering momentum.

Sleep came in fragments.

When I did sleep, I woke often. Not from nightmares, but from vigilance. My body did not trust unconsciousness. It felt like abandonment of duty. I learned how to wake quietly. How to lie still and assess the room before making a move. How to control my breathing so it wouldn't give me away.

These were not dramatic moments. They were repetitive. Ordinary. Invisible. And repetition is what shapes a nervous system.

By morning, I was tired in a way that did not show. I moved through the day feeling functional, composed, and praised, even for maturity, responsibility, and being "so good."

No one asked what it cost.

It was in those nights—wide awake, heart racing—that I began to sense a presence that felt different. Steady. Familiar. Safe.

I didn't have the language yet to call Him Jesus. But I knew I was not alone.

The pendulum swung to love bombing for a while after my sister left. I almost believed things might actually be different now. Almost.

We were a religious family. Church attendance was nonnegotiable. My mother eventually became the Director of Christian Education. From the outside, we looked devout. Inside, faith felt structured but distant— what some might call the "frozen chosen." Doctrine without intimacy. Ritual without refuge. Requirements, but no relationship.

Still, the seeds were planted. I knew the Bible and its stories, even if I didn't know Him. Or, at least, I didn't know that I knew Him.

Even though the environment was unsafe, something in me recognized safety when it brushed past.

Looking back now, I can see the pattern clearly. There wasn't one event that put me in the grave. There were many. Small cuts. Repeated cuts to my soul and my mind. Cuts that didn't bleed enough to alarm anyone, but bled just enough to teach my body that the world and the people in it were not to be trusted.

Over time, something solidified.

I did not think of myself as wounded. I thought of myself as capable. I could absorb discomfort. I could endure awkwardness. I could take a hit—emotionally, physically, socially—and keep moving.

People began to rely on that. They leaned on me. Trusted me. Expected me to manage what others could not. I did not yet see that as a problem.

I saw it as proof that I was strong. However, strength built this way comes at a cost. It teaches you to ignore signals. To override instinct. To confuse endurance with health. To believe that needing less is the same as being resilient.

By the time I reached adolescence, the grave had already taken shape—not as an event, but as a posture. A way of being in the world that assumed pressure was normal, and relief was temporary.

I had not yet found a name for it.

I only knew how to live inside it.

I learned to function.

I learned to perform.

I learned to endure.

And I learned—quietly, efficiently, without conscious thought—how to bury parts of myself that needed tenderness in order to survive.

That is how graves are made.

Not all at once.

But patiently, as the vulnerable parts of you that engage and connect stay hidden to facilitate protection.

And by the time you realize you're in the grave, you realize you made your bed there long ago.

"Therefore prophesy and say to them, 'Thus says the Lord God, 'I will open your graves and make you come up out of your graves, My people; and I will bring you [back home]....'" — Ezekiel 37:12 (AMP)

When Telling the Truth Made Things Worse

I learned early that telling the truth does not always lead to protection. Sometimes, it makes things worse.

In my parents' bid to build excitement for another move, they talked to us about Denver, what it would look like, and when. We even pulled the encyclopedias and the atlas off the shelf to cast vision and dream together. After all, in my family's timeline, we'd already stayed longer in the Kansas City area than we had anywhere else. I was so excited. No one had told us it was a secret. They talked to us about it as if it were done, or mostly done. So, I was excited to tell some of my best friends, who told their parents.

Secrets are a big thing in my family. A solidly known family rule: don't air our dirty laundry...or else. I didn't think this qualified as 'dirty.' So when my friend's mom called my mom to offer congratulations. I was most definitely not prepared for the verbal evisceration that would follow. My grave was dug a little deeper in that moment as I died to myself in new ways while I listened to my mother tell Jennifer's mother that I was a liar.

She didn't imply I had a strong imagination. She didn't say I was confused or misunderstood, nor did she offer cover or take ownership of the 'misunderstanding' regarding our conversations about moving. She named me a liar. Who is an adult going to believe, the 'adult' mom or the child? My mother verbally eviscerated me when she got off the phone. I remember she did, but I honestly don't remember what she said. I was numb.

I no longer knew what to believe. My family's specialty is next-level gaslighting; the casualty in this war is the inability to trust oneself. This would initiate a decades-long struggle to seek and advocate for the truth alone. Even though I knew what had happened and what had been said, I began doubting myself, which was worse than doubting my mother. My mother would often make up things for me to believe and promote to others as truth, while simultaneously looking for the moment to expose the falsehoods. Remember the earlier story where she made me believe I had brain cancer? It was an exercise in insanity that, had the Lord not been on my side, probably would have succeeded in me losing my mind or my life completely (Psalm 124).

None of my friends at school believed I hadn't lied about it. None of my friends at school forgot that my own mother declared me to be a liar. The irony is that in my family, this is probably most likely due to my CPTSD, which, in an effort to continually provide opportunities to process the events, allows for perfect recall, whether bidden or unbidden. Like a looped reel in my head, I am the truth teller whose mind refuses to indulge the lies. To make matters worse, my dad didn't get the job. We didn't move. And there was no way to prove what they'd told a ten-year-old child. This is just one of many stories that highlight this part of the 'game' I unwittingly played with my mother. While I may have been gaining a bit of momentum here and there in the power imbalance, she always had an ace up her sleeve to knock me right back down.

It wouldn't be until high school that I finally got the courage to seek help from the school counselor. It was not a strategic decision. It was not bravery. It was exhaustion. The kind that comes when carrying something alone becomes heavier than the fear of what might happen if you speak.

I had reached the point where holding everything in felt more dangerous than letting something out. I told the counselor, an older woman who wore no makeup and sensible shoes, what was happening at home.

I didn't dramatize it. I didn't embellish. I told it plainly, the way children do when they haven't yet learned which versions of the truth are acceptable. I remember watching her face as I spoke, gauging whether I had miscalculated again—whether this, too, would be minimized or dismissed. I didn't have much experience sharing the truth about what happened at home or my feelings in general. It broke the primary family rule: *Don't air our dirty laundry.*

She listened.

At least, it seemed that way, but there is a difference between hearing and listening. I was only fifteen. I not only had to transfer schools in August when I entered a huge high school with thousands of students, but we were no longer able to attend our high school in our area because my sister, who had been kicked out, had gone there (my parents' mandate). The system there knew too much about our family, so we moved again, if only to different school districts, not houses. I also had just had the traumatic surgery during Christmas break, and my face drooped slightly on one side until the nerves rerouted. I had lost any love for my mother and felt the final plunge of the knife of betrayal in a sucking chest wound that just seemed to fester in my soul.

I poured my heart out in a trauma dump. Then...I was sent back to class. Unnatural silence after the storm was the norm, so I didn't think much of it. Being able to concentrate in class, though, would prove too hard a task.

What I did not know—what I could not have anticipated—was that my words did not stay in that room as protocol demanded. She called my older brother into her office. She told him everything I had said. When he denied it, she believed him. When I got home, he threw me against the garage and held me up by my neck, and with his finger an inch from my face admonished me for *airing our dirty laundry*.

The next day, with faint bruises still visible on my throat, the counselor told me that nothing good could come from repeating made-up stories of my mother's mental illness. The message was clear: silence was safer than truth, and loyalty mattered more than reality.

What stayed with me most was not what was said in that room, but what happened after it.

There is a particular silence that follows betrayal. It is not empty; it is charged. There is an energy begging to be released. It follows you down hallways and into classrooms. With no outlet, it settles into your body like a residue that cannot be washed off. I remember walking back to class feeling as though the floor had tilted slightly—nothing dramatic, just enough to make balance unreliable.

My body responded before my mind could sort out why. My shoulders lifted and stayed there. My breath shortened. I scanned faces for signs that something had changed, that something had leaked out and taken on a life of its own. When nothing obvious happened, the absence of evidence did not reassure me. It heightened vigilance. Waiting for the threat I could not yet see to emerge.

I learned something in that aftermath that would take years to unlearn: telling the truth does not guarantee protection; it guarantees exposure. Exposure without care teaches the nervous system to retreat even further.

I did not feel angry then. Anger requires safety to be fully expressed. I felt careful. I learned how to navigate the rest of the day without drawing attention to myself, how to minimize my presence, and how to contain what had been stirred up inside me. The cost of having spoken lingered long after the conversation ended.

My interpretation of that moment birthed an institutional rule written into my being: Truth is punishable. But, in a family of gaslighters, being a truth teller became my mission. The only lifeline to cling to, like the only working compass in the midst of a lost voyage.

The system that was supposed to protect me reinforced the same message I had learned at home. Do not speak. Do not expose. Do not disrupt the appearance of 'normal'.

I came vulnerable, seeking help and support. Instead of protection, I was redirected.

I was placed in Forensics class (not forensic science, like CSI, but forensics as a competition for prose, poetry, and improv; the yang to the yin of competitive debate).

At the time, it may have seemed like an elective class change. A creative outlet. A neutral decision. Emotionally, it was something else entirely. Being redirected did not feel like an opportunity. It felt like containment.

On paper, the change looked benign—an adjustment, a scheduling solution, a way forward. In my body, it registered as something else: a narrowing of options designed to keep things quiet. I learned that systems smooth disruption not by addressing it, but by relocating it to a less visible place.

I adapted quickly. Adaptation had always been my strength.

Performance became a sanctioned means of existence. I could speak without saying what mattered. I could express emotion without naming its source. I could be seen without being known. The rules were clear and, in that clarity, oddly comforting.

But comfort did not equal safety.

The skills that helped me survive at home translated easily here: reading the room, modulating tone, and understanding what was expected without being told. I learned how to hold attention without inviting scrutiny, how to participate without provoking consequences.

This was not freedom. It was a refined version of silence.

Acting rewarded the very skills survival had already taught me: reading people, managing emotion, performing believability, disappearing into roles that were safer than being myself. I learned how to use my voice without using my truth. How to express emotion without plumbing the depths.

Performance may have become a sanctioned means of existence, but something unexpected happened there, too. Through acting and forensics, I encountered one of my first gifts along the way, Sally Shipley. It's always the people who make the difference, good or bad, and the 'good' ones are the gifts we collect that are a beacon when we lose our way, and the tempest threatens to pull us under.

By then, I had learned not to expect adults to respond well to honesty. I didn't trust authority figures. I didn't seek out mentorship–I didn't even understand that concept. I stayed alert, cautious, and contained.

Mrs. Shipley did not ask me to explain myself. She did not interrogate my story or ask me about my late admission to her class that year. She did not require disclosure to offer dignity.

She simply saw me, just as she made it a habit of seeing all her students. Her classroom was a safe haven, even while she insisted on our best and never lowered her standards. She taught us to not only find our voice, but insisted we use it confidently...no matter how long or how much practice it took.

She treated my intelligence as something worth cultivating, not something to manage or subdue. She invested in me as though my presence in the room mattered—not because I had earned it, but because I was worth it, just for being human, and all she assumed was inherent in that.

That assumption was radical. Radically kind.

In her classroom, I experienced something unfamiliar: authority that did not punish truth, space that did not demand silence, and expectations that did not require self-erasure. The difference was not intellectual. It was physical.

I noticed it before I trusted it. The moment I stepped into her classroom, something in my body softened, surprising me. My shoulders dropped slightly. My breath reached lower. The constant internal scanning—so automatic I rarely noticed it—paused.

It wasn't relief. Relief implies expectation. This felt more like a peaceful disorientation.

At some point, I remember a shift had happened. While sitting at my desk, I was no longer rehearsing what I might say if called on. I was listening instead. Not waiting for threat, not calculating response—just listening. The absence of urgency felt almost unsafe at first, like letting go of the steering wheel on a road I didn't know.

My nervous system did not immediately trust this. It watched closely. It waited for the correction, the snap, the moment when safety would reveal itself as conditional, and ironically, too risky.

It didn't come.

Being treated as though my presence was expected—not managed—was unfamiliar. I had learned to measure myself constantly against invisible lines. Here, the lines were visible and fair. That clarity did not exhilarate me. It unsettled me.

Because once your body experiences a different way of being, returning to vigilance is no longer neutral. It becomes a choice you make because you believe you have to.

I didn't yet understand the language of attunement or psychological safety, but my body recognized it instantly. The vigilance softened. The constant internal monitoring eased just enough to take a breath. Such a foreign concept to me.

This was not a rescue. It was contrast.

Mrs. Shipley did not undo what had happened. She did not reverse the cost of telling the truth. What she did was expose the lie that I was the problem. That being honest was inherently dangerous. That I was too much or too sensitive, or too disruptive. I was always too much or not enough in alternating measures, so the axiom of just being myself was lost on me, but she gave me space to try.

Her presence introduced new possibilities:

That some authority could be trustworthy.
That my voice could be uttered without negative consequence.
That intelligence and creativity were valuable and could be nurtured rather than punished.

And once you have seen those possibilities, you cannot unsee them. Returning to silence after that felt heavier. More conscious. More costly. I did not suddenly become free. But something in me shifted.

The grave no longer felt all-encompassing or like a foregone conclusion. There were whole chunks of time I didn't feel hopeless. And the silence that once felt like safety and beckoned me to remain began to feel like a choice I never knew I had. I couldn't name it at the time, but while I sat wrapped in grave clothes, the seeds of *awareness* began to break open, determined to burst forth from the ground as tender shoots that would eventually blossom in their time.

"The wilderness and dry land will be glad; the desert will shout in exultation and blossom like the autumn crocus. It will blossom abundantly and rejoice with joy and singing..."
— Isaiah 35:1-2 (AMP)

CHAPTER 5

Bully Slayer

The grave does not erase instinct.

It sharpens it.

By the time my sister left, something in me already knew the rules of survival, even if I didn't yet know how to articulate them. When she looked at me and said, *"Don't ever let her hit you again. Don't let anyone ever hit you again,"* it didn't feel like a call to courage. It felt like a warning delivered too late.

That sentence did not land as encouragement. It landed as responsibility.

I carried it the way children carry things they are not meant to hold — without context, without training, without relief. It did not come with instructions or protection. It simply arrived and stayed, echoing in moments when fear surged, and decisions had to be made quickly.

I did not yet know how to keep myself safe. What I knew was that *someone had named a line*, and once named, it could not be unnamed. Even when I crossed it poorly. Even when I froze instead of standing. Even when I hid.

The sentence followed me into rooms and hallways and nights when I lay awake listening. It did not make me brave. It made me aware. And awareness, once awakened, does not sleep easily.

She wasn't giving me a strategy.
She was naming a line, which I now know is a boundary.

For a long time after that, I didn't cross it. I circled it. Measured it. Tested it from a distance. Survival still meant retreat.

When my mother's anger began to move through the house, it announced itself long before it arrived. There was a sound to it — a cadence in her steps, a weight in the air. My body learned to respond before my mind did. I went to my room and did what I had learned worked.

I closed the door.

Then I reached for the blue Barbie doll suitcase and the red baby doll travel trunk and slid them under the door handle — one wedged just right, the other angled for resistance. It wasn't dramatic; it was mechanical. I was waiting for someone bigger and stronger than me to fight the battle. Like Rapunzel waiting for the prince that never came. There would come a time I would have to fight the battle myself, but that time had not yet come.

I sat on the floor with my back against the door, feet braced, listening. The act itself was quiet, almost reverent.

I remember testing the angle of the suitcase with my hands, adjusting it slightly until the resistance felt right. I remember noticing how the door handle pressed into the plastic, how much pressure it could withstand before slipping. I learned more about leverage in those moments than I ever would in a classroom.

My body learned before my mind did: survival is not always loud. Sometimes it is precise.

Sitting there with my back pressed against the door, I did not pray for her to stop. I prayed for time. Time for the house to change its mood. Time for my father to come home. Time for the moment to pass without escalating into something worse.

Fear did not feel dramatic. It felt procedural.

Listening for her voice outside.
Listening for the test of the handle.
Listening for the sound that mattered most — my dad's car pulling into the driveway.

When I saw it, I threw the window up and yelled for him. I told him I was stuck. I told him I wasn't coming out until he came for me.

And... he shushed me.

Not because he didn't hear me, but because "what would the neighbors think?"

That shushing did something permanent. It taught me that my pain was negotiable, but embarrassment was not. That being harmed could be tolerated, but being seen could not. That silence was not just a coping mechanism — it was an expectation.

I internalized that lesson quickly.

It followed me into classrooms, friendships, churches, and eventually adulthood. The instinct to lower my voice when things became uncomfortable. The reflex to contain instead of confront. The awareness that visibility always came with risk.

I learned how to speak just loudly enough to be understood — and never loudly enough to cause a scene. That moment settled into my body with a clarity I wouldn't name for years: safety was negotiable, but appearances were not. Silence wasn't just a coping mechanism. It was a rule.

After that, the physical outbursts slowed, but the threat didn't disappear. It learned new shapes. I learned the limits of hiding.

I finally realized no one was coming to rescue me. I was eight years old when the moment came to slay the bully on my own. Try as I might, I don't remember the spark that lit the flame that set her off. I do remember the too-familiar look of rage in her eyes as I ran and she chased me. Knowing I couldn't win this game, I grabbed the kitchen phone and dialed 9 and 1 because hiding wasn't going to work this time. I don't remember deciding. I had been taught about 911 at school for times when you feel in danger or unsafe. I remember standing in the doorway, the phone heavy in my hand, my heart racing ahead of my voice. I said — out loud with a voice I scarcely recognized, but where she could hear me — that if she came closer, I would dial the other 1.

I wasn't daring her.
I was introducing a consequence.

She told me I wouldn't do it. She told me I didn't know what abuse was, but she did and recounted her own childhood abuse. She told me they'd take me away, and I'd come crawling back. She told me I was ungrateful.

That's what bullies do when you disrupt their momentum — they make the cost sound worse than the harm.

But she stopped. Not in surrender. In recalibration.

I didn't feel victorious. I felt hollow. Sitting alone at the dining room table afterward, phone still in my hand, I understood something that would become a pattern: even when resistance works, there is often no repair. The house did not feel safer afterward. It felt quieter in a way that required vigilance.

No one came to sit beside me. No one asked what I needed. No one explained what had happened or named it as wrong. The phone returned to its place on the wall as if it had never been lifted.

I learned that using my voice did not guarantee care. It guaranteed consequence.

That realization did not send me back into silence. It made my silence more calculated. More selective. I began to understand that speaking up was a tool — one to be used carefully and rarely, because the cost was always higher than I expected, even though it was sometimes worth it.

Silence returns — but now it carries weight. And this woman was still in charge of me, and the moments when I didn't have enough air to breathe.

My dad was on a business trip. I'm not sure where my older siblings were, but when they returned, no one asked about the strange silence because it had become normalized in our house. And, if they did notice a shift, they didn't want to know its source.

After that moment, she largely quit parenting. She went back to work for the first time in my life. Then went to school forty-five minutes away to pursue her Master's. I was in the unique position to have my dad take me to doctor's appointments and even cook dinner, which the oldest set of siblings never experienced. He was present, and he never used his words or his body for violence. Still, I would spend an inordinate amount of time trying to get his attention or any engagement. He was stoic and emotionally unavailable, which made my room a place of safety for an entirely new set of reasons.

When it came to decisions, my mother was still in charge. As a child who struggled mightily with breathing. I often wouldn't get permission to go to playdates or birthday parties because there was no guarantee there wouldn't be cigarette smoke (inside or outside), or pets, or running, or, and I'm not kidding, kids laughing and "cutting up." If I did go, I had to try desperately to have no trouble breathing before or after the event. Slumber parties were rare, but not never. You might think that this is just an overprotective mother looking out for my best interests. Sure, you might be right if, when I struggled breathing, she didn't withhold not only love, but also delayed medication, or worse, berated me the whole time I took the medication.

At night, if I had trouble breathing, I would wait and hope and pray it would go away or get better, even though there was close to a 100% track record of me not making it to morning without intervention in such cases. By the time I walked into my parents' room and stood at my mom's side of the bed, all I could do was pat her arm to get her awake because I was long past the moment when I had air to make any sound come out. She would then scold me for whatever I had been doing that day. "If you hadn't been laughing, this wouldn't be happening to you." "I saw you cutting up with your friends." "I told you you shouldn't go to that [insert play date] with your friends." If silent tears betrayed me and rolled down my cheeks, she'd start anew. "It's too late for that. Don't start that, you'll only make it worse." As if it were my fault that a throat narrows closed when crying and sadness take hold.

She also made me go to the pharmacy with her to pick up my prescriptions. She would tell me how much money they'd spent on my doctors' bills and medications just to keep me alive, and all they could be doing or have if it wasn't for me. My dad wasn't moved by much, but she knew she could get a rise out of him if we returned, and she mentioned that the costs or prescription prices had gone up. I learned to hate the idea of money being spent on me. I learned to dissociate during moments and enter one of the worlds from my books. I learned I was always too much, or quite simply not enough, unfortunately, always over things I couldn't control. My existence was a burden for which I tried hard to demonstrate had no effect on me.

Though I collected bright moments and positive people as gifts along the way, the truth was that the world outside the house wasn't gentler.

My trauma had taught me I could enjoy the glimmers of joy, but wait with bated breath for the other shoe to fall...because it would.

At school, my body marked me as a target before I ever spoke a word. High-dose steroids for my lungs had given me a "moon face" when I was in an acute phase, and kids noticed. A boy from my brother's class, Scott, noticed. After recess, while he held the door open for all of us to walk past, he puffed his cheeks out as I passed, laughing with his friends. No adult intervened. I learned how humiliation travels deeper when no one names it.

What stayed with me wasn't his face — it was the laughter behind it.

Laughter spreads responsibility thin. When everyone is laughing, no one feels accountable. The cruelty becomes ambient, part of the environment, something you're expected to adapt to rather than resist.

I adapted.

I learned how to maintain a neutral expression. How to move through hallways without looking up. How to swallow the impulse to defend myself because experience had taught me that defense often made things worse.

Each swallowed response felt small on its own. Together, they shaped my posture in the world.

Scott and his friends were gone into junior high by the time I hit fifth grade, but I traded one set of humiliation for another. This is about the time the years-long sinus infection began that would lead to surgery. A teacher told me I could blow my nose in the hallway whenever I needed to. Not because I was sick, but because the kids were making fun of me when I blew my nose. The solution wasn't to stop the cruelty. It was to move me out of sight.

Walking into the hallway with tissues in my hand felt like being politely erased. No one accused the kids of cruelty. No one told them to stop. The responsibility shifted entirely onto me — to manage their discomfort by removing myself from sight.

I remember standing there, listening to the muffled classroom sounds through the door, understanding something quietly devastating: accommodation was expected of the wounded, not the ones doing the wounding.

That lesson repeated often enough to become instinct. That lesson lodged deep: the problem isn't harm; it's visibility.

Elementary gym class brought its own theater of exposure. Oh, Gary was a horrible gym teacher. I mean, in the traditional sense, he might have been fine. As a human capable of compassion or empathy, he failed miserably. Rather than include me anywhere he could, he let it be known he thought I was a faker (disregard the thirteen medications and numerous trips to the nurse's office each day for their administration). Being called a faker did not anger me as much as it confused me.

My body was already fighting to breathe. My life already involved medications, nurse visits, and missed activities. The accusation wasn't just untrue; it erased my lived reality. A reality I couldn't imagine anyone choosing if they had a choice.

I began to understand that authority did not require accuracy to operate. It required compliance. And I had already learned what happened when you refused it.

Gary decided that, rather than letting me participate in every activity I wasn't restricted from, he had a rule: if anyone couldn't participate in warm-ups (i.e., running, jumping, etc.), they wouldn't be allowed to participate in the main activity. All I had learned to date was that, regardless of location, any adult or child could treat me however they wanted. My feelings didn't matter, and, in fact, how I felt was wrong, not their behavior.

I learned that adults rarely caught bullies; sometimes they were bullies themselves, but they were excellent at exploiting weakness. The neighborhood taught me the same lesson.

The neighborhood boys, who were the same bullies at school, ensured I knew a figurative blow could come at any time. Generally, the neighborhood kids, especially right by our house, were good. I grew up in the Golden Age of playing until the street lights came on. If I'm honest, other than my next-door neighbor, Becky, and one other neighbor behind us, they were mostly my brother's friends, and I was the tag-along. If we rode bikes, I was sometimes allowed. If we were on foot, most likely no - the whole no running clause and all.

However, around the corner were a couple of bullies who had aggressive dogs to match. We avoided that street at all costs. The dogs weren't hard to avoid, but the boys were another story. It didn't matter what I wore (which is a whole story for another time; we weren't even allowed to wear jeans until well into my teenage years, not because of religious reasons or any good reason, just control). They would make fun of me. I literally have no idea why. I kept to myself. They didn't know me. I just seemed like an easy target, and they saw me shrink, which I guess was the objective that gave them power. Through my post-graduate education in psychology, I came to realize the reasoning and the power imbalance in these moments. But, as a child, I was just a girl in elementary school trying to survive.

It took me years to learn how to hold verbal and mental abuse at bay. There was no moment of mastery, just repetition, error, and adjustment. Then my sister — the one who had left — came back briefly when I was eleven as a single mom of a toddler and now a newborn.

I had idolized her. Believed she was different. Safe.

One afternoon, her toddler wandered into the room where I was watching TV and began crying the way toddlers do. I tried to soothe him. She stormed in and accused me of hurting him, which just isn't in me and certainly wasn't in any capacity at the time.

Something in me snapped — not explosively, but cleanly.

I saw it then: she was just as broken as our mother, mirroring the same patterns. The protector I had longed for since she was forced to leave six years prior was capable of the same harm. As an eleven-year-old, it was like a dam broke within me, and I saw the truth for what it was. She was as broken as any of us and, for sure, just as broken as my mother, whom she was emulating. I learned there was really no one to trust.

That realization stirred something within me. And for the first time, I railed back — shaky, honest, refusing the lie. The quieter, demure me, who had shrank in the face of verbal abuse for so long, simply railed back at her with the truth. The hurt that she, my protector, would refuse the truth in favor of lies to malign me was untenable. I shouted back at her, albeit shakily. She and my mom were verbal masterminds. I was proud that I stood up for myself, even though I'm sure she didn't see it that way, if she even considered the moment at all.

That was another kind of slaying. Not confrontation for dominance, but truth spoken without permission.

This newfound confidence to slay bullies, other than my mother, carried over into sixth grade.

I had a teacher known for being cruel who singled out students verbally. Some thought she was just strict, but she lacked grace and compassion, creating an environment that thrived on 'Gotcha!' moments. I was known as being quiet up to that point in school. I shrank, not drawing attention. Something new shifted, revealing part of my foundation that would never be shaken. When the teacher picked on another student, something in me — trained by years of watching injustice — refused to stay quiet. I spoke up.

This new pattern of behavior shocked her–and me. I was sent into the hallway. Then to the principal. Breaking a cardinal rule: *don't escalate*. I walked to the principal's office exuding a confidence I did not yet feel, certain the trouble at home would far exceed anything the principal could muster.

What I learned also shocked me. My mother may be mean and used to beat the hell out of her own kids, but she'd be damned if anyone else did. Hmmmph. Who knew? She not only stood up for me, but demanded change for the class. I often wonder how different our lives and the world would be if she had healed and learned to channel all of that energy for good.

The teacher was fired mid-year. And replaced with someone kind. That wasn't a fairytale ending, but it was a revelation. Children are the most unempowered demographic, and that day, a girl who had spent years calculating danger learned something irreversible: there is only one way to slay the bully, whether from inside your own camp or without, call their bluff, and stand.

This is the truth about becoming a "bully slayer." Resistance did not make me popular. It made me legible.

Teachers watched me more closely. Peers avoided me or tested me. Adults labeled me difficult instead of discerning. Each boundary I tested came with a social cost.

And yet, something essential remained intact. I did not disappear. I did not always win. I did not always stand. But I stopped folding automatically. I learned that fear did not mean I was wrong — only that something mattered.

The exception did not undo the rule. If anything, it made the rule more visible. I could now feel the difference between spaces that required silence and spaces that did not. That awareness changed how I moved through the world. It made compliance feel heavier and resistance feel more necessary.

But necessity does not equal readiness.

I carried the memory of safety like a fragile object—something to be protected, not exposed. I did not yet know how to build it for myself. I only knew how to recognize it when it appeared and grieve when it disappeared.

That grief did not slow me down. It sharpened me.

And it set the stage for what came next: a gradual, uneven refusal to disappear quietly again.

It wasn't a moment. It was an accumulation of experience born from trauma.

Hiding behind doll suitcases.
Listening at the doors.
Yelling out windows.
Dialing 9 and 1.
Swallowing humiliation.
Testing boundaries.
Paying for it.
Testing again.

I didn't become fearless.
I became unwilling to disappear.

That posture kept parts of me alive when I was hopeless. It also kept me braced for danger, hypervigilant, pacing the wall to keep the enemies out. If that practice also kept friends out, then it was a price that would have to be paid. My brain had already been rewired for protection instead of connection.

Standing takes energy. Standing alone takes more. I hadn't yet learned how to stand in the Lord's strength or utilize the tools He gives us to battle. And when you stand alone in your own strength long enough without rest, without safety, without repair — the body keeps score.

I didn't know it yet, but resistance had limits. There would be plenty of times to find out I was not invincible, and my body would be the one to tell me.

"My flesh and my heart may fail, but God is the rock and strength of my heart and my portion forever." — (Psalms 73:26)

CHAPTER 6

The Weight of Standing

"How long, O Lord? Will You forget me forever? How long will You hide Your face from me?"
— Psalm 13:1 (AMP)

I kept standing.

Not because I was okay, but because standing was what I knew how to do. It was the posture my nervous system trusted most—upright, alert, prepared. By college, I could sell "normal" convincingly if you didn't look too close. Years of putting white wash on our family's story had taught me how to do damage control when the mask had slipped for a moment. I knew how to do public relations. I knew how to keep the scarlet "A" hidden.

And then one day, my family made it impossible to keep hiding.

My sister, who is six years older, showed up at the sorority house without warning. Surprise visits, in my experience, are rarely good things, as anyone with CPTSD will tell you. I was in my room with my two roommates when someone let her in and walked her right back to us unannounced.

She didn't sit down.

She didn't hug me.

She didn't soften her voice.

She didn't say, *How can I help you process this?*

She simply blurted it out—like a grenade tossed into a room and then abandoned.

"Our mother has been locked up in a psych ward involuntarily. She was suicidal."

No preamble. No context. No details. She had no other information. And she was gone in two minutes—turned and left me standing there in stunned silence with my roommates and the truth hanging in the air like smoke.

Shock does not always feel loud. Sometimes it feels like the sudden loss of gravity.

I remember standing there, watching as the words hung in the air, while my roommates' faces changed in real time. Eyes widened. Bodies stiffened. No one knew where to look. I could feel the story becoming *public* before I had even touched it myself.

I did not cry. I did not ask questions. I catalogued reactions.

That was my reflex—to track the room before attending to my own body. To measure how much of this would spill beyond the walls and how quickly it would do so. The part of me that had learned public relations early kicked in immediately, trying to contain damage that had already escaped.

My sister had already turned to leave. There would be no follow-up. No explanation. No checking in later. She delivered the truth the way people deliver bombs—quickly, decisively, and without staying to witness the aftermath.

Once she was gone, silence returned. Not the safe kind. The kind that waits for someone else to speak first. Familiar ground, the aftermath of the storm, surveying the damage. I learned then that some truths do not bring relief when they are finally named. They simply rearrange the room.

No public relations magic could cover over this one.

No one present could pretend they hadn't just heard all of that, especially me. It wouldn't be the last time I would desperately want to turn back time to erase the hard moments. Mostly, they tried anyway— eyes sliding away, bodies turning, the awkward shuffle of people who don't know what to do with someone else's family hell.

One roommate finally asked, wide-eyed: "Oh my gosh. Are you ok?"

I'm always ok.

Except I wasn't.

Since the surgery my freshman year of high school, I had told my mother I hated her rather than loved her. It wasn't a dramatic proclamation. It was a fact that settled in when love had been worn down to something unrecognizable. And now I had no idea what was happening. I only knew my three sisters had her committed.

So I did what my younger self had learned to do.

I called my oldest brother to ride in and save the day.

My dad had left my mom, albeit temporarily, after the whole affair debacle, and they were newly entering the empty-nester phase. That was enough to tip her over the edge, and she ended up in a version of the same place she had sent my sister fourteen years earlier—different facility, same concept. My dad wasn't available to talk or help, or work through this. I'd wanted him to leave her for a long time, as if that would solve anything. For a moment, I tried to tell myself maybe this was a good thing. But I was too numb inside to know what I felt.

Numbness is not peace. It's being paralyzed with a pulse.

College doesn't pause for your family crisis. Professors don't rearrange syllabi because your childhood finally became public. I had to do damage control with my roommates. Navigate time with my professors. Show up to group therapy sessions where the focus was solely on her well-being, not ours. Go to a hearing to consider her sanity.

And all of it exposed a truth I didn't want to admit: I could not keep doing life the way I had been. I couldn't keep pretending I was good at STEM classes for pre-med, and carry this too. So I switched majors to journalism with a minor in French. I was in triage, and my hopes and dreams had to take a backseat to the sucking chest wound that was still my mother.

Then came *the* moment that should have been *my* moment to put my mother on trial in the courtroom.

The judge wanted to know my assessment of my mother from my perspective. In my mind, it felt like she was finally on trial—the bully I had "slayed" in one way, but in other ways still hadn't. This wasn't a trial; it was a hearing. But emotionally, it felt like my chance had arrived. The moment where truth could finally be named in a way that mattered.

I wanted to tell him everything.

The monster she could be. The lies. The damage. The way she had killed parts of me through death by a thousand cuts.

And then I looked at my brother—the same brother who had told me not to say the truth.

And I honored the family rule.

We. Do. Not. Air. Our. Dirty. Laundry.

With tears betraying the sacrifice of my inner child's voice on the altar of my mother's freedom, I lied. I said I didn't think she should be kept and wasn't a harm to herself or others. The truth became stuck in my throat, desperate to escape utterance, but was denied.

The hearing should have been the moment truth mattered most.

I remember sitting there, listening to clinical language describe a woman I had lived with my entire life. Symptoms were named. Behaviors categorized. Risk assessed. It all sounded orderly—neat in a way my experience had never been.

Then the judge looked at me.

The question was simple. My answer could have been devastating. I felt the weight of the room shift, the way it does when authority waits for confirmation. This was the closest I had ever been to telling the truth in a way that carried consequence.

And I didn't.

I looked at my brother. I remembered the rule. *We do not air our dirty laundry.* I felt my inner child's voice recede as my adult mask snapped into place.

I lied. Not dramatically. Not maliciously. Efficiently.

The lie did not feel like betrayal in the moment. It felt like obedience. Like maintaining the system I had learned to survive within. I did not feel relief when it was over. I felt hollowed out.

Truth had been invited—and I had declined.

That choice did not end the crisis. It extended it.

When she was released, my brother took her to the East Coast to live with him—true to his word. I thought he meant forever. It was only a few weeks or months. Then he declared her well, brought her back to Kansas City, and then he returned to the East Coast.

I expected something to change once she was gone.

Distance often masquerades as resolution. But absence did not heal what had already shaped us. When she returned, she was declared "better," but the system reset without addressing the damage underneath.

I was left holding two truths at once: What I had endured was real. And nothing about it would be repaired.

That realization did not free me. It hardened something. I learned that acknowledgment does not guarantee care. That naming does not require healing. That systems can confirm reality without offering protection.

And still, I kept standing.

I went back to classes. Completed assignments. Showed up. Smiled where necessary. Carried on conversations that felt disconnected from the life I was living underneath them.

Standing had become procedural.

I had grown up watching adults manage crises poorly. Now I was expected to manage *them*.

There is a particular loneliness that comes when the people you once believed would step in cannot—or will not—do so. I felt it settle into my chest as I realized no one was coming to tell me what to do, how to feel, or where to stand.

I was in college. I had exams. Papers. Responsibilities that did not pause for family implosions. The world did not widen to accommodate this moment. It narrowed.

My father's absence landed heavier than I expected. I had imagined, for years, that if the truth ever surfaced fully, he would finally step forward.

That something would be named and addressed. That acknowledgement would bring change. It didn't. The truth was, he knew more about her reality than any of us, and it had never moved him.

Instead, I was left holding information without authority and grief without permission.

Standing shifted again.

It was no longer just resistance or vigilance. It became coordination. Managing logistics. Managing perception. Managing what was said and what remained unspeakable.

I learned how to compartmentalize at a professional level. That is what standing looked like in college: Not triumph. Not healing. Damage control. Silence was chosen again, even when truth was finally invited.

And after all of that—after the psych ward, the hearing, the lie, the whiplash—I still kept standing.

The summer after this, I really didn't want to stay at home. I felt I had worn out my welcome at friends' houses in summers past. I attempted to secure a legitimate summer staff internship with a mega church and other parachurch organizations, but they believed I was too messy for formal discipleship training (as a seminarian, I can now recognize the flaws in that theology). Then two of my college friends felt called to serve on their own summer staff in the inner city and needed a female counterpart. I said yes to the inner city, not because I was whole, but because I knew how to function in chaos, was hungry to grow spiritually, and didn't want to be at home for the summer. We were supposed to live in a tag house between two rival gangs. We moved to the church across the street because it seemed safer. It wasn't safe—just safer. They were so gracious to us and what God did through us.

We had no training, no oversight, no guidance, no backup. We walked through the neighborhood and spread the word. On the first day we opened our doors, two hundred children were lined up in front of the three of us. I learned what a fish-and-loaves moment looks like when it isn't a story you read—it's a line of hungry faces you can't ignore.

A thirteen-year-old girl who, in addition to being raped by her mom's boyfriend, was left to care for twin five-year-old sisters, began staying with me. She was there because she didn't want to be home. I knew what it was not to want to stay home. When the police said she could no longer stay, I found confidence and strength I didn't recognize. I think it was the tipping point of all the injustice I experienced and witnessed welling up inside. It was the spark that lit the flame, demanding that adults and authority figures take care of children, the most unempowered demographic.

With a blind rage, I walked down the street, barging into the drug house where her mother was, passed two guards with assault rifles, and demanded she come out and be a mother to her girls for no other reason but that they were worth it.

To my utter surprise, those present in the drug house agreed with me and told her to go take care of her girls, effectively throwing both of us out of the house.

I made it back to the curb in front of where I was staying, and my legs turned to jelly, refusing to cooperate. I dropped down and wept— because somewhere deep inside me I knew I had just stood up for her the way I once wished someone would have stood up for me.

When the summer ended, and I left, that thirteen-year-old girl was mad at me for leaving "like everyone else." Years later, she told me what it meant that someone had seen her and stood up for her.

And still, I kept standing. I may get knocked down or drop from the weight of it all. But, eventually, I stand again.

Her tears as I left burned in my brain as I left to return to college for Rush Week. My own tears blurred my vision, and I felt my efforts were futile, a drop in the ocean of injustice and despair. Since we were unofficial, there was no oversight. No debriefing. No processing or guidance on how to assimilate back into college after such a summer.

Once again, I was left in the silence that ensues after trauma. Standing, surveying the damage, and figuring out how to put the pieces back together and go on.

I refocused my efforts as a corporate warrior with a commitment to myself to abandon outreach. At this point in my life, I deemed the vulnerability and empathy required to come alongside those hurting to be too much. At this time in my life, I had no resolution for my own hurt and didn't find a ready solution for theirs either.

By the time this chapter of my life closed, I had learned how to do something very well. I could hold competing realities without dropping either. I could function while fractured. I could manage a crisis without collapsing. I could tell the truth selectively and survive the consequences.

This did not feel like strength. It felt like a necessity.

I did not yet know that standing this way exacts a price that is always deferred. That the body, patient and precise, keeps its own record. That weight accumulates quietly until something finally gives.

For now, standing still worked. And that was enough to keep going.

I finished my last year of college, graduating in three years, and then I met Darin.

"But I'll take the hand of those who don't know the way, who can't see where they're going. I'll be a personal guide to them,

directing them through unknown country. I'll be right there to show them what roads to take, make sure they don't fall into the ditch. These are the things I'll be doing for them—sticking with them, not leaving them for a minute." — Isaiah 42:16 MSG

CHAPTER 7

Standing, Until the Body Breaks

"If any of you lacks wisdom, let him ask God, who gives generously to all without reproach, and it will be given him." — James 1:5 (ESV)

I did not stop standing when I met Darin. Standing *beside* Darin did not mean I knew how to lean on someone else or even collaborate with them in life.

There is a difference between companionship and safety, though I didn't yet have language for it. We could occupy the same space without flinching. We could hold conversations that didn't require pretending. We could acknowledge brokenness without needing to solve it. That alone felt rare.

But I did not yet know how to be held without scanning for collapse.

Love arrived without instruction. It did not quiet my nervous system; it activated it. I learned how to stay vigilant, even in intimacy, and how to brace for disappointment, even in moments of connection. Standing *with* someone felt safer than standing alone—but it was still standing.

And standing was all I knew how to do.

I met him from the same posture I had learned to live from—upright, alert, braced. I did not come to him healed, whole, or at rest. I came practiced in endurance, fluent in vigilance, capable of holding my own weight, and more.

He did not enter my life as a rescuer. He entered as someone who could stand in unresolved terrain without flinching. There was steadiness there, but not safety. Familiarity, but not peace.

And, there was a lie.

He told me he was a Christian.

Learning that Darin had borrowed faith rather than lived it did not break something between us but exposed something already fragile inside me.

I had been raised to treat faith as currency: something you prove, perform, or protect. Hearing him claim an identity he hoped to grow into felt uncomfortably familiar. I recognized the posture immediately because I had used it myself: claiming strength before I felt it, claiming trust before I understood it.

The fracture wasn't that he lied, the fracture was that truth still felt negotiable in places where I needed it most.

So I stayed alert.
I stayed observant.
I stayed standing.

I believed him—not because the claim rang true in some deep, settled way, but because I wanted it to be true. Faith had always been part of my life, even when it wasn't a refuge. The idea that we shared that language mattered more than I realized at the time.

Later, I would learn the truth.

He wasn't lying maliciously. I think he thought he was a Christian, as far as checking boxes go. He was borrowing an identity he hoped would eventually fit. But borrowing faith isn't the same as having your own faith, and the lie is still a fracture when truth is what you need most.

Something in me registered that fracture immediately—not as betrayal, but as confirmation of something I had learned early: Even the good things require vigilance, looking for how to protect myself for what *may* come.

I stayed anyway. Standing had taught me how.

We planned an almost fairy tale wedding. I couldn't imagine everyone not being as happy for me as I was for me. But the same sister, who had also been engaged and married several times, didn't want a fairy tale for me. Her daughter, my niece (yes, that niece), who stayed with me in the sorority house, in my brand-new apartment, and in every house I lived in later, was six, on the verge of being seven. She and I were close, and she was the obvious choice to be the flower girl.

My mother flew in from New York to get the dress and see the venue. She was only in town for a few days, and we made the most of our time together. I had no idea how to forgive her, but I desperately wanted to have a normal family, even if it was only pretend. It turns out that moving out of state helped perpetuate that delusion immensely. Maybe we would have had a 'normal' day, except, we were going to the venue on the same day my sister was celebrating my niece's birthday. We were never going to miss the birthday party or any part of it. She meant the world to me, so why would I? But my sister flew off the handle, like so many slamming doors on so many celebration days before. And that perfect fairy-tale day I was planning happened without my niece as the flower girl and without the one sister I had asked to be a bridesmaid. I'll never forget the tears on her little face as I was forced to walk away from her birthday party, much the same as her mother did to me when she was kicked out when I was five. The repetitive cycle of trauma is hard.

Marriage did not pull me out of the grave. It simply gave me a companion inside it. We stood side by side. Two hurting souls, both of us carrying histories we did not yet know how to lay down.

Then our first daughter was born.

She lived!

I held her in my arms and felt something open that terrified me more than anything that had come before. Love arrived without armor. Responsibility arrived without instruction. I had never loved anything or anyone this much in my life. It was terrifying and spectacular.

Holding her did not calm me.

It magnified everything.

I felt the weight of generations in my arms, the things I knew I did not want to pass on, the patterns I feared I would repeat simply by existing inside them. I did not trust instinct. Instinct had been shaped in unsafe places. Not trusting myself was a new kind of hypervigilance, in which I became part of the problem.

I remember studying her face and thinking, *I do not know how to do this without hurting you.*

That thought did not come from a lack of love. It came from honesty.

I had learned survival. I had learned resistance. I had learned endurance.

I had not learned gentleness.

Begging God for wisdom was not an act of faithfulness—it was an act of fear. I was afraid that without divine intervention, history would outrun intention. That desire alone would not be enough to protect her. That love, without framework, structure, and healthy function, could still cause harm.

And so I asked God for help. I knew, instantly and with absolute clarity, that I had no map for this. I did not have a model for how to mother without harm. I did not have a picture in my mind of what safety looked like inside a family. What I had was a catalogue of what *not* to do and the unshakable fear that, left to my own devices, I would repeat the trauma.

I remember holding her and thinking, *I am going to mess this up.* Not because I didn't love her, but because love had never been enough to prevent damage where I came from. So I did the only thing I knew how to do when I reached the edge of myself. I begged God for wisdom. Not performatively. Not eloquently. Desperately.

I clung to James 1:5 the way a person clings to a lifeline: *If any of you lacks wisdom, let him ask God...*

I lacked wisdom.

I lacked a blueprint. I lacked confidence. I lacked precedent.

And so, I asked.

That prayer did not make me calm. It did not suddenly make me certain. But it anchored me to something outside my fear. I did not yet trust myself, but I trusted that God was not asking me to do this alone. He'd been the only constant in my life, and I had to stake *her* life and my legacy on the promise that He would not leave me or forsake us.

Unfortunately, trauma loves the comfort of what it knows. My parents had moved to New York within a month of my graduating from college. With the birth of Jessica, they moved back. Not only back, but in with us. What was supposed to be temporary ended up with a traumatic exit two and a half years later.

Two and a half years of my mother telling me what a horrible mother *I* was. She thought she could cover over the past by doing things "right" with Jessica, as if she even knew what that meant. To accomplish that, she apparently needed to portray me as a bad mother and told Jessica and me that at every turn. Always when my dad and Darin weren't around.

We kicked them out of our house and eventually their influence out of our lives. But in the interim, I stood again. Motherhood did not soften my posture—it sharpened it.

Responsibility multiplied without reducing fear. I watched myself more closely than I watched her. I monitored tone, response time, discipline, affection—searching constantly for signs that I was becoming what I had sworn I would never be. Sometimes the effort blurred with reality as default patterns die hard.

I did not yet understand that hypervigilance could masquerade as care. I believed that if I stayed alert enough, intentional enough, vigilant enough, I could outmaneuver harm.

Standing became a maternal instinct.

Then, in the midst of the joy of being a young family of three and having space to breathe again. Loss came back.

Pregnancies that were lost far too soon, but still too late to not be devastating.

Miscarriage is a quiet devastation. It does not crash into your life; it drains it. It arrives through sonograms, appointments, and lab results, and phrases meant to comfort that land like static.

We were led into the sonogram room, a room I would become very familiar with, for both good and bad reasons. There was no heartbeat. I begged them to check again. It had to be wrong. It must be wrong, because didn't they know all things were working out well for me? They must not have known. I am a daughter of the King! You have to check again. The sonographer left to get the doctor. I told the doctor it was wrong. She said it wasn't. I told her about my faith, which could move mountains, and my God, who could restart heartbeats. Give me the requisite three days!

She begrudgingly relented. I was too far along to deliver myself, and she didn't want complications. We drove home, and I believed with absolute certainty that God would come through for me. My mother felt the need to chime in that this was obviously God's way of saying Jessica should be an only child. She, who had lost a child shortly after birth. She, who had six children, was saying my daughter should be an only child, and God was orchestrating death.

I withdrew and prayed for three days straight. The day arrived for the procedure at the hospital. I believed it would be declared a miracle, and we would walk out. I insisted on a sonogram being given before going back to the OR. They indulged me. I began sobbing when no heartbeat appeared on the screen. I have never felt such utter rejection. How could God have let me down? Why would he forsake me? I would later learn that if Jesus could ask that from the cross, then I can too in my own moments of despair.

The doctors were quick to put me to sleep. But the moment I awoke, the most unholy wail escaped my lips that I almost didn't recognize as my own voice. Though I'd been through much, I had never experienced this level of torment. The God of the Universe, whom I trusted, I felt utterly rejected by in my time of need, and I gave up. How was He any different than my earthly parents or anyone else who had rejected me? I had already seen Him at work, seen too much to doubt His existence or ability. However, my limited theology and everything I had read or thought I knew didn't help me understand this pain, which felt like a personal attack. So, I wept, and wept, and wept.

There is no socially acceptable posture for miscarriage.

It is not public enough for a ceremony and not private enough to remain invisible. People do not know what to bring. There are no scripts that fit. Grief lives in the body and has nowhere to go.

I learned how to grieve efficiently.

I learned how to fold loss into routine. How to return phone calls. How to answer questions without inviting more. I learned how to stand in the presence of people who wanted reassurance more than truth.

And each time, something inside me went quieter.

Not numb, but thinner like fragile ice on a newly frozen pond.

Thank God I already had Jessica; otherwise, I'm not sure I would have had the motivation to get out of bed again. My mom, showing her true colors, doubled down on this being God's will, especially that Jessica should be an only child. She might have waited a few days, but eventually she expanded her explanation to include the idea that if I were a better mother, I would have more children. I wish I had gone through healing to stop the noise and not agree with her. I wish I had learned to create a peaceful space that disallowed and disinvited those who threatened it. But I just hadn't healed that much yet. It seems ridiculous looking back or seeing it objectively, but it was all I ever knew.

You may be wondering what Darin had to say about all of that. Well, I was desperate to keep him from finding out I wasn't really a good mom. Apparently, he bought it because he told me and everyone else that I was a great mom. She never said those things in front of my dad or husband. They didn't know, though I'm sure my dad suspected, that I was emotionally tortured. They only knew I cried and couldn't quit, and assumed it was hormones.

Each time, I gathered myself and kept going.

I did not scream at God.
I did not walk away.

But something thinned. The ice threatening to crack day by day under pressure

Standing before God with empty arms does something to faith. It doesn't shatter it; it exhausts it. The theology I had leaned on—obedience rewarded, endurance yielding fruit—began to lose its shape.

I prayed again.
And lost again.

Repetition changes grief.

The first loss asks *why*.
The next asks *how long*.
Eventually, the question becomes *how much can a body hold before it starts to give way?*

My prayers became shorter—not because I had less faith, but because words felt insufficient. I prayed with my hands open and my expectations guarded. I wasn't postured to receive so much as begging Him to take the grief and stress from me. I did not stop believing, but belief no longer felt buoyant.

It felt heavy.

Standing before God with empty arms did not feel rebellious. It felt confusing. Like speaking a language I still loved but no longer understood.

And, loss came again, this time mixed with victory. And that was even more disorienting.

This time, I was pregnant with quintuplets. I was pretty neurotic with this one, understandably. Once again, the ultrasound room would be a proving ground. When we found out we were pregnant with quintuplets...what? Wait, that's five. Yep. Since the last miscarriage, I hadn't had regular periods, so the doctor thought low-dose Clomid would help me regulate. Well, it did help me ovulate because now I have five fraternal 'twin' babies to carry. That got me to a perinatologist. Unfortunately, no sooner were we told we had five babies in there than another ultrasound would have me reading the sonographer's face for a look I knew all too well.

I was already praying and bargaining with God not to let it be the case. The doctor came in and lowered her face to an inch of mine, which was facing the wall, willing this not to be my reality. She said low and firm, "You have one heartbeat still beating in there. You will not stress out. You will give this baby everything you have right now. Let this be your sole focus." The good news was that I had one baby still fighting, so I did too. The bad news was that I translated the doctor's admonishment to forget the four I was carrying whose hearts beat no more. And that was hard.

I stuffed the emotions down in a way that I know, now as a psychologist, is very unhealthy. Every time I wanted to grieve or cry, I felt guilty for the one who remained because the negative emotions and stress might harm her. I didn't know how to process it. Back then, I told very few people about losing four and still having one. It was a very confusing time, marked by a rollercoaster of emotions. Those who did know didn't really know what to say or do either. Also, I lived with the moment-by-moment anxiety of wondering if this survivor was moving too much or not enough.

I remember driving to work and stopping at the traffic light at the hospital. I had been praying and offering up my mustard-seed-sized faith to God (Matthew 17:20), because it was literally all I had left. Between working at the hospital and going to see the perinatologist and my regular OB, I had sonograms every week and often multiple times a week. My OB would have me come in around lunch and say, "Let's wait til the sonographer goes to lunch, and we'll sneak in. She'll never know." I'm sure the sonographer did know, but if it was booked, I would have to be charged. They were ridiculously kind to me. Although I would be hospitalized halfway through and placed on bed rest, which continued at home later, Sarah Faith made her way into the world. She was stuck; her birth was hard, but she fought valiantly to survive. So I did too.

Grief stacked without ceremony. There were no rituals that fit. No language felt sufficient. I learned how to function around it the way I had learned to function around everything else—efficiently, quietly, without letting it slow me down.

I thought we were done with children. The trauma and drama of pregnancy were too much. A year after Sarah's birth, we had to divorce my family to carve out some semblance of space to heal and grow so that I could change a legacy. All such hard work to continue standing when the grave beckons for me to lie down permanently.

On two separate forms of birth control, and nursing with the last one, I got pregnant twice more, with them being only a bit over a year apart. Grace Ana's birth was late, and my body crashed, literally, during her birth, requiring the crash cart and five shots of EPI. Gabriella "Ella," the second half of the dynamic duo, rounded out the four...the tribe. Her birth caused a hemorrhage, and the declaration from my OB that we were done.

By then, my body had already begun to whisper its limits. Fatigue that didn't resolve with sleep. Pain that lingered without explanation. A constant hum of tension that made stillness feel unsafe.

However, I had learned how to override signals, and having children is a great way to divert attention away from oneself.

Then the interruption came, and standing was no longer an option.

"I will lead the blind by a way they do not know; I will guide them in paths that they do not know. I will make darkness into light before them and rugged places into plains. These things I will do [for them], and I will not leave them abandoned or undone." — Isaiah 42:16 (AMP)

CHAPTER 8

Stillness

"Be still, and know that I am God."
— Psalm 46:10 (NIV)

I did not decide to stop. That distinction matters.

Stopping had never been part of my vocabulary. Rest had always felt like negligence. Stillness felt suspicious. I had learned to stay upright through silence, resistance, loss, love, motherhood, grief, and faith that kept thinning without breaking.

So when standing finally ended, it did not come as surrender. It came as removal. A sort of mental and spiritual parallel to the physical amputation doctors were recommending.

The shopping cart did not appear to be dangerous. I knew from experience that danger often comes disguised, hence the need for hypervigilance and shrewd eyes that discern the truth. Here, it did not announce itself, and tragedy occurred through no fault of my own. If it is my own reckless decision, then at least I would have been empowered to change the trajectory. But it's the unexpected trauma on repeat that lends itself to CPTSD.

In fact, here it was a shopping cart designed for children, complete with taxi-cab features and thick plastic sides and steering wheels. It did not carry symbolism or warnings of danger. It was ordinary—metal, wheels, momentum—moving through space the way things do every day.

One moment, I was walking. Next, I could no longer stand on my own.

The sound came before the pain—a wet, unmistakable tear, followed by blood where blood should not be. My body registered the rupture before my mind could catch up. I knew immediately that this was not a sprain. Not a strain. Not something that could be walked off with grit and denial. My foot was limp at the ankle, and pumping significant blood onto a hot grocery store parking lot while all four of my girls watched in horror.

There is a split second when the body knows before the mind can argue.

I remember the sensation not as pain first, but as wrongness—an immediate, unmistakable signal that whatever had just happened was not something I could negotiate my way through. The ground felt farther away than it should have been. Sound arrived late, distorted, as if I were underwater.

I tried to stand. The instruction went out from my brain. The response from my body never came.

Blood pooled in a way that did not look accidental. It had direction. Purpose. I remember staring at it and thinking, *This is not a mere scrape.* The clarity was calm, almost clinical. Shock has a way of organizing thoughts before it steals them.

People moved around me. Voices asked questions that required answers I could not yet form. Someone told me not to look. Ha. I was never afforded the luxury of looking away from the carnage. I'm the one who staunches the bleeding and leads crisis control. The body does not forget what it witnesses at the moment control starts to slip

Stillness arrived before anyone had a chance to say the word.

My leg did not respond, but the rest of me still could. I must, for them, stay calm. Stay calm. Someone called an ambulance, but I refused. There was no chance I was leaving my babies with anyone. Except that one niece, whom I called to come.

Shock has its own quiet. Time slowed. Voices blurred. The world narrowed to the space between my body, my children, and the ground. I would not faint, no matter how much blood I lost. Darin was on call at another hospital thirty minutes away with other people clinging to life. They were depending on him to save them, so I couldn't. I had learned long ago to stand alone, but here, standing was no longer an option. And I felt alone.

At the hospital, language took over, rewriting my story with plot twists I did not want to walk through. Traumatically severed Achilles tendon. Damaged nerves. Nicked arteries. Compromised blood flow. The words landed clinically, efficiently, without regard for what they meant in the context of a life already lived, braced and hanging on by a thread.

Medical language does not soften impact. It categorizes. It compresses. It translates a person into systems and probabilities. Tendons, nerves, arteries—each named with precision, each reducing my future into a series of clinical contingencies.

I listened the way I had learned to listen to authority—attentive, quiet, already bracing for what would be required of me. I asked practical questions. I noted timelines. I measured expectations. What I did not do was imagine myself not standing.

The possibility hovered unspoken. It felt impolite to acknowledge. As if naming it might invite it closer. So I stayed focused on logistics: surgery schedules, transportation, childcare, and the choreography required to navigate the next few days; my mind was not yet ready to acknowledge that it would, in fact, be weeks turning into months, and then years.

This was not denial. It was habit. Forced stillness does not ask permission before it begins.

Surgeries followed.

Surgeries failed.

Then more surgeries.

Skin grafts failed, too. Circulation remained tenuous. Infection loomed. Each appointment carried the same undercurrent—*how bad is it today?* A gaping hole was still prominent on the back of my ankle, requiring daily attention.

Eventually, about seven months after the accident, the word entered the room.

Amputation.

It was spoken gently, as if tone could soften the meaning. As if removing a part of me would simplify things. The metaphor for my visible body, aligned with my invisible mind and spirit, was rich and profound. There are several parts that should be the subject of amputation that have failed to heal. They spoke as if adaptation to missing parts would be easier than repair, and many doctors and therapists claimed it would.

When the word entered the room, it did not sound dramatic. It sounded efficient.

Amputation was presented as one option among others—a way to simplify, reduce risk, and make the future more manageable. It was spoken by those who were tired of the continued work my healing would require. The tone was gentle, almost reassuring, as if discussing the removal of a part of me could be done without emotional consequence.

I refused immediately. Not with a speech. Not with emotion. With certainty.

The refusal surprised even me. It came from the same place my earlier refusals had come from—the place that had learned survival through resistance. Saying no felt familiar. Comfortable. Safer than surrender.

I did not yet understand that refusal had been my primary strategy for staying alive. Stillness was not something I trusted.

Again, I refused the amputation. Not because I felt brave, but because I knew, given half a chance, I would fight and *somehow* find a way to stand. Not just stand, but stand whole and made new. Sure, I know plenty of people with physical injuries who thrive and stand tall with prosthetics. This wasn't about logistics for me. This was an inner battle manifesting outwardly.

However, what followed was not recovery. It was confinement.

One final last-ditch effort through surgery to close the hole in the back of my ankle involved bringing over a surgeon from Stanford to assist my own surgeon. They were hoping, and I believed, before going under anesthesia, they would rebuild the inner structure with mesh and then eventually add skin grafts. What I woke up to was fire on the back of my thigh. Searing pain from a large skin graft harvested to cover a reverse flow sural artery flap that would forever disfigure my leg and still not guarantee I would walk without assistance, but at least there would be no gaping hole...IF it took.

I was admitted on bed rest. *Again*. For weeks. This time, with my leg in traction and zero privileges to sit up, much less to stand.

Wheelchairs and assistive devices replaced walking and independence. The world shrank to what could be navigated seated. Stairs became obstacles. Bathrooms required planning. Getting dressed became an exercise in humiliation and patience. In a house that wasn't ADA accessible, this meant crawling to care for children.

I learned the layout of my home from a seated position. I memorized which surfaces were reachable and which were not. Independence became conditional, dependent on the availability and patience of others.

I hated the waiting. Waiting to be helped. Waiting to be moved. Waiting to be finished with this chapter.

Time slowed in ways that did not feel restorative. Days blurred together, marked not by accomplishment but by repetition. Medication schedules replaced routines. Pain management replaced momentum.

Stillness was no longer theoretical. It was enforced. My body was no longer something I could rely on.

Not even six months after this surgery, another bomb was dropped. This time, the C word entered the picture. A concerning axillary breast lump drew all the attention, defied biopsy norms with indeterminate results, and left them determined to excise the tumor.

My body rebelled at the thought of one more surgery. My mind refused to believe there wouldn't be a last-minute way out. Yet, the excision happened, and while they were in there, they removed five axillary lymph nodes *just to be sure.*

No cancer. Just more scars.

Then, a week out, I went back for the check-up and told the surgeon something was wrong. He didn't believe me and might as well have patted my head and told me to run along home. Twenty-four hours later, my husband called him from his own hospital shift, believing something to be gravely wrong. Obviously, he believed *him.* My surgeon said if I come in to get checked, we'll both be home by midnight. He lied.

It was the threat of an ambulance that prompted me to call my niece to come get me. It's interesting how she was always one who would come. I had to wait until she dropped off her mother, my sister, who is 10 years older than I am, at her brother's house from the airport, because my sister insisted I was just seeking attention to detract from her holiday visit.

I never made it out of triage to a room. Straight to the trauma OR they opened up for emergency surgery. My temperature was over 105 degrees and climbing by the time surgical sleep once again claimed my mind.

Not wanting to miss Christmas with my girls, I was released from the hospital. Darin had to meet his parents halfway to get the girls; they didn't want to bring them all the way up, and I couldn't travel. Because Darin is a doctor, I was released to his care for Christmas, even though I had an open wound in my chest that my daughter would have to help him pack and repack each day.

There was no cancer. But scars and lymphedema would require a new set of physical therapists. It's weird being the only one in the cancer physical therapy clinic who doesn't actually have cancer. A type of survivor's guilt nudged me, but I was too numb to embrace it.

Then I had to get back to the business of relearning how to walk. Three physical therapists quit on my "delusion" that I'd ever walk again without assistance. When the therapists stopped believing progress was possible, they did not say it cruelly. They said it clinically. My goals were unrealistic. My persistence was misplaced. They did not frame it as a failure. They framed it as realism. The implication was clear: *accept limitation and move on.*

I had heard this before.

Authority has always been comfortable telling me what I could not do. I listened, nodded, recalibrated. Compliance had kept me alive in other contexts. It felt reasonable to apply it here.

And yet, something inside me resisted—not loudly, not defiantly, but stubbornly. The same stubbornness that had carried me through years of standing refused to concede this ground.

Stillness did not mean surrender. Not yet. Accepting *"no"* had never been my strength.

A fourth therapist believed. So I worked.

I dropped my children off at school and treated rehabilitation like a full-time job. Hours of repetition. Pain without progress. Setbacks that felt personal, even when I knew they weren't. The work was relentless, thankless, and isolating. Getting a glimmer of response from dead nerves in my foot proved trying. I worked on mirroring the two feet, willing the right foot to cooperate.

Standing returned slowly. First with assistance. Then with effort. Then with exhaustion. At first, it was an effort without grace. Movement felt foreign, like borrowing a body that did not quite belong to me. Each step required concentration. Eventually, I walked again. Then ran. Then climbed mountains. Each gain arrived with fatigue rather than celebration. People called it progress. From the outside, the story sounded like resilience. Inside, it felt like restoring a semblance of balance. Because standing again did not undo the posture I had learned. My nervous system did not register recovery as safety. My body remained vigilant. Even upright, I stayed braced for impact. I had learned how to rise without learning how to release.

Recovery did not bring relief. It brought vigilance in a new register. My body no longer trusted itself. I no longer trusted my body. Movement required monitoring. Balance demanded attention.

Even when I was upright, stillness remained close. It waited.

And when the doctors, therapists, and onlookers declared me "better," something in me knew the truth: I was functional. I was not free. Stillness did not come with the injury alone. It came with what followed.

The slow realization that my world could no longer be held together by willpower. That my body had reached a limit my mind refused to acknowledge. That every strategy I had used to survive—standing, resisting, enduring—now required a cost I could not afford.

There were days I lay awake at night, staring at the ceiling, unable to sleep, not because of pain, but because stopping felt like falling. When you have lived upright for so long, stillness feels like disappearance.

Stillness is not restful when it arrives by force. It strips identity quietly. Roles dissolve without ceremony. The metrics by which I had measured myself—productivity, usefulness, resilience—fell away one by one.

I could not show up the way I had before. Could not carry others. Could not absorb chaos. Could not override fatigue.

I did not collapse dramatically. I simply could not keep going. That is how *The Grave* ends—not with death, but with incapacity. Not with despair, but with silence. I did not yet know what would come next. I did not yet have language for calling, meaning, or response. For the first time in my life, endurance was not an option available to me. There was nothing left to negotiate. No posture to adjust. No strategy to deploy.

The body had spoken. But rather than a death knell, it was a call to lay down all I had known. To acknowledge what wasn't working, believe I had been created for more, and to come forth to something new.

"Come to Me, all of you who are weary and burdened, and I will give you rest. All of you, take up My yoke and learn from Me, because I am gentle and humble in heart, and you will find rest for yourselves. For My yoke is easy and My burden is light."
— Matthew 11:28-30

The Calling

"Since God's gracious gifts and calling are
irrevocable." — Romans 11:29

CHAPTER 9

An Invitation to Destiny

"Before I shaped you in the womb, I knew all about you. Before you saw the light of day, I had holy plans for you: A prophet to the nations—that's what I had in mind for you." — Jeremiah. 1:5 MSG

This verse has always undone me. The idea that God knew me—really knew me—before anyone else ever did has been the anchor in seasons when I've felt unseen or misunderstood. As the sections' titles indicate, we switch from the grave to the calling, but there's so much overlap it's hard to know where to mark the line. I wish I could say the healing and growth were linear, but grief and trauma ebb and flow like the tide. I developed grace for myself along the way, a quality I wish I had known how to extend to my current self and past inner children who helped me through. If you're on a healing journey, remember to be kind to yourself. This sacred work is hard stuff. At the time, I didn't yet see it, but God was already weaving threads of my calling through the broken pieces. My heart for being a light to the lost, for defending the vulnerable, for speaking when others stayed silent—it was all quietly taking root even as I was still trying to heal.

Healing was anything but linear—more like waves rolling in and pulling back, sometimes calm, sometimes crashing without warning. If you're new to your journey and discouraged by feeling one step forward and two steps back, please be encouraged today that you're not failing. It's not hopeless. The seasons still ebb and flow. One day, you too will look back with hindsight and declare, "Look what the Lord has done!" Remember to raise Ebenezer's (1 Samuel 7:12) along the way; they make it easier to spot the times the Lord has helped in the valleys from high-up places.

Though this next section is titled "The Calling", expect to find times of willingly and unwillingly walking back into the grave, tending to the grave of that which I left behind, and moments of walking in freedom and clarity as I gained healing and wisdom. It's a messy, wonderful process. If you're in a place of not knowing what to do and feeling like you're at the end, celebrate! You're in the prime place of dissatisfaction where you'll long for, pursue, and find God as you seek Him with your whole heart. What a sacred journey.

I did not leave the grave and step into clarity. In fact, I didn't really leave the grave for a long time. I made one decision at a time. I took one step toward the light, then sometimes, two steps back toward the misery I knew.

God's gifts and callings are irrevocable (Romans 11:29). I'm grateful for His patience and His promise to use all things for good (Romans 8:28), especially for the moments in my life I had yet to call *good*.

We discuss two types of calling; both are applicable in this section. I was called to come forth out of the grave. To refuse to stay stuck in the learned helplessness of unhealthy thoughts and behaviors, similar to the man Jesus asked if he wanted to get well in John 5:3-9. There is a call to come out of the grave into integrated health and healing.

Then, there is also our life's Calling. An assignment that merges our lived experiences with our faith and education to contribute something to this world that impacts others positively.

That distinction matters because the story you are about to enter is not one of sudden understanding or spiritual epiphany. It is not a story of being rescued from pain or rewarded for endurance. It is a story of attention—slow, embodied, often uncomfortable attention—and what happens when a life that has learned how to survive finally stops running long enough to be still and know.

What you have just walked through was the formation of a posture forged in the grave.

The posture of standing. Being knocked down and standing again.

Standing when silence was safer than truth.
Standing when resistance was costly.
Standing when faith thinned, but obedience remained.
Standing when love arrived without a map and responsibility multiplied without rest.

Standing was never heroic. It was necessary.

The grave was not a single event. It was an environment—built over time through repetition, adaptation, and the quiet acceptance of conditions that were never meant to be permanent. It shaped how my nervous system learned to respond, how my body learned to brace for impact, how my spirit learned to endure without asking too many questions.

The grave taught me how to survive. It did not teach me how to heal. The grave can only hold what is dead. Exiting the grave requires healing and speaking life to resurrect that which has long been dead.

Healing requires a different posture. And that posture cannot be forced. Refinement occurs when we're called out of the grave, because facades and all that white washes what is dead in us become exposed to the light. What is dead belongs in the grave. It cannot come with us. Even though we may long have wished to be free from its hold, we've grown used to the weight of our dead parts. Leaving them behind is a grieving process and can be disorienting. I was tempted to revisit what I had left, to wrap the known misery around me like a security blanket and lie back down in the grave.

But once I heard my name called to come forth out of the grave, I simply couldn't resist it. I could ignore it for a while, but the grave cloak never fit quite right after that moment.

If *The Grave* was about what happened to me—and what I learned to do in order to keep going—*The Calling* is about what happens when going with the status quo is no longer possible, and we must go through birthing pains to emerge reborn from the dark place.

This section will revisit certain moments you already know.

You will encounter familiar scenes, relationships, and seasons again—but not because they need to be explained further or justified. They will be revisited because healing does not require new facts; it requires a new lens.

What changes in this section is not the story—it is the **orientation**.

Trauma embeds itself not just in memory, but in the body.
Beliefs are formed not just through thought, but through physiology.
Faith is lived not only in conviction, but in regulation, attachment, and trust.

Where *The Grave* traced the roots that shaped my internal environment, *The Calling* begins to tend it through pruning and grafting into the vine that is the Source of life.

This is where the work shifts from endurance to integration.

From a posture of standing in defense to sitting and listening.
From reacting to responding.

From surviving to becoming curious about what survival has cost—
and what healing might make possible, even thriving.

The calling did not arrive as a directive. It did not sound like a voice
telling me what to do next, or where to go, or who to become. It did not
come with a timeline or a sense of confidence. In fact, it arrived precisely
when confidence was no longer available to me.

It came as a question.

Not a theological question.
Not a moral question.

A practical one.

What do you do with a body that no longer cooperates with your will?
What do you do with a nervous system trained for threat when threat is
no longer immediate?
What do you do with faith that has endured, but not yet rested or
learned to fully trust?

What do you do with a life that has been lived almost entirely in reaction
rather than proaction or response?

The calling did not ask me to explain my suffering or redeem it. It asked
me to begin moving towards healing, which, ironically, required me to
be still and listen. And then, it asked me to be brave enough to feel what
trauma had told me was not safe to process and had kept stored for
'later'. The calling asked me:

To stay with my body long enough to hear what it had been saying all
along.
To stay with my emotions without converting them into
responsibility.
To stay with my faith without forcing it to perform certainty.

This is where healing begins—not as an outcome, but as a reorientation in how we process and interpret life. Mind, body, and spirit do not heal independently of one another. They are not separate systems that can be addressed in isolation. The body remembers what the mind has forgotten. The nervous system resists what the spirit has not yet learned to trust. Belief settles where safety allows it to land.

In *The Calling*, you will see how healing unfolds not through effort, but through alignment.

You will see how receiving becomes as formative as doing. How safety becomes a prerequisite for transformation. How attention reshapes identity. You will also see how calling does not erase the grave, because it is there. All of that trauma really happened to us, and in some respects, there is no undoing what has been done. However, the transformation out of the grave recontextualizes everything.

Nothing in this section minimizes what came before. Nothing bypasses grief, loss, or the reality of what it costs to live in a body shaped by trauma. Healing does not pretend the grave never existed. It composts the trauma to enrich the soil, where life can grow and bloom, and where festering wounds can heal. Scars remain, but they serve as a roadmap and a testament to surviving that gave way to thriving.

This is where neuroscience and Scripture begin to intersect—not as competing explanations, but as converging truths. This is where faith becomes embodied. Where prayer changes shape. Where the nervous system is invited into a rest it has never known.

This section will be slower. More reflective. Less event-driven.

If *The Grave* asks you to stand and be vigilant, *The Calling* asks you to sit, then move with purpose.

To notice what you feel when there is no longer a task to complete or a threat to manage. To pay attention to what rises when the noise subsides. To recognize how much of life has been lived in reaction—and what might be possible when reaction gives way to response.

The calling does not demand that you be ready or have it all figured out to come forth out of the grave. It meets you where readiness is no longer required, but presence and intentional progression are hallmarks of the change in location.

What follows is not a formula. It is not a prescription. It is a testament to the slow, layered work of healing—work that unfolds at the intersection of presence, biology, and belief.

This is where the shift begins. Not forgetting the grave, but thanking it for what it taught us, and bringing those lessons with us into the light and into a new season.

"But from there, you will search for the Lord your God, and you will find Him when you seek Him with all your heart and all your soul." — Deuteronomy 4:29

CHAPTER 10

Learning to Sit in Stillness

> *"Our fathers sinned; they no longer exist, but we bear their punishment." — Lamentations 5:7*

The stories did not need to be told again. CPTSD ensured it played like a loop in my head, unbidden and unrelenting. What needed to change was how I was holding them. How I processed them. How I interpreted them. And, my posture with them.

In *The Grave*, I learned how to stand. Standing was not symbolic. It was necessary. It was how I survived motherhood without a blueprint, grief without ceremony, faith without rest, and marriage without safety. Standing meant staying functional. Standing meant being ready to respond. Standing meant not collapsing when collapse would have been reasonable.

But once I stopped moving, perhaps prowling is more apt, once stillness was no longer optional, I began to realize something unsettling: I had never *listened* to my life story. I had only managed it.

Sitting did not give me new memories or erase the life I'd lived. But it did allow me a new vantage point. My soul-healing journey and therapy provided me with new tools that allowed me to step back and view things from a neutral observer's perspective. From a 30,000-foot view, I could feel safer processing what I had already lived through—without adrenaline, without urgency, without the need to prove that I was okay.

My heart and soul couldn't produce a different outcome for my brain, but I was being transformed by the renewing of my mind through the process (Romans 12:2).

Huge life-altering events, like Motherhood, sounded different when I sat with them.

When I held my daughter and thought, *"I am going to mess this up."* I had always understood that thought as humility, as a sense of responsibility, as love taking its weight seriously. Sitting with it revealed something more precise. I had not been afraid of failing as a mother. I had been afraid of instinct itself. Instinct had been shaped in unsafe places. I did not trust what rose automatically in me and didn't want to perpetuate the trauma.

The title "legacy changer" wasn't part of my vocabulary. I had no framework or structure to describe the shifts and tenacity with which I would embark on soul-deep work to change my children's experience. I didn't know it yet, but my *Calling* would include being a legacy changer. I didn't feel like an agent of change at the time. I didn't feel equipped. I didn't feel ready. If anything, I felt more vulnerable than I ever had, holding that newborn that was my and my husband's sole responsibility. I only knew I wanted–not exactly *more* than I had per se, but also yes, more. I wanted more peace for my children. More guidance. More stability. More equipping. MORE LOVE! Except, I didn't feel I possessed any of those things myself.

So I compensated.

I monitored myself relentlessly—tone, response time, discipline, affection (and not necessarily adequately, especially at first)—not because I lacked love, but because vigilance had replaced trust long before I knew their names. Sitting helped me realize that what I had called devotion was often fear masquerading as responsibility.

I had begged God for wisdom. I had clung to James 1:5 like a lifeline. I lacked a blueprint. I lacked confidence. I lacked precedent. Sitting did not invalidate that prayer. It clarified it. I asked for wisdom because I had no idea how to love someone so deeply. I had seen hundreds of ways not to parent, but not one right way to do so. The prayer was faithful—and protective. Both were true.

And, I grieved for the loss of my childhood. I grappled with what it was to love my infant babies before they took their first breath, willingly giving my life for their own, and considered my own mother, a bully I had to slay.

I didn't yet sit with my inner children, the versions of me that got me through so many tough times and still stood, waiting to be heard. Waiting to be held, to be comforted. I hadn't heard I could do that, but at this point, I wasn't ready for that step either. I simply sat from my view on high and tried to see them, really see them, and what they'd gone through...what *I'd* gone through.

At this point, I allowed myself to cry for them, but not with them. Like a tragedy played out on the big screen that moves us to tears, I shed plenty of tears for their story as an observer. I was not yet asked or invited to come alongside them and make their stories my own. That would come. For now, it was enough to sit, watch, listen, and observe their experience through their eyes without engaging or absorbing.

Events like loss and grief, so much loss and grief, were the hardest to shift perspective. It felt like rejection and betrayal. However, they also gained new significance when I stopped standing over them.

For instance, in *The Grave*, I wrote that there is no socially acceptable posture for miscarriage. I learned how to grieve efficiently. I learned how to keep going. Sitting did not reopen those losses–they'd never closed. It allowed me to hear what the repetition of loss had done to my body.

What the compounded effects of seemingly unanswered prayer had done to my spirit.

Standing before God with empty arms had not shattered my faith. It had exhausted it. I had not walked away. I had not screamed. I had not stopped believing. I had adapted. Sitting, let me admit that endurance had come at a cost. Prayer had become quieter, not because it mattered less, but because words could no longer carry what my body already knew.

As I took steps into my calling outside of the grave, I began to realize I can hold two truths simultaneously. I can grieve loss and still celebrate joy...without guilt. The joy cannot cancel out the grief, but neither should the grief overshadow the joy. During the healing process, I began to bear witness to the good and bad aspects of my childhood. If it were all bad, well, that would almost make sense. But the truth is that there were moments of joy I didn't get to fully embrace because my young mind and body had learned to brace for impact. Nevertheless, there were joyful moments during that period. Both were true simultaneously.

Another expression of this dichotomy is Sarah's birth. I lost four babies on the heels of two miscarriages, and yet, I held Sarah Faith. A fulfillment of a promise and an answered prayer. A rainbow and sunrise baby. Grief and joy held equally in my heart, but not in my arms.

In the Grave, I shoved unwanted emotions behind lock and key, lest they come out and ask for attention. Now, from my bird's-eye perch, I could zoom out and first observe casually what had happened. Who were the people involved? What were each of their roles? And, what was their impact on me in this moment?

Marriage also revealed itself differently when I listened.

I already wrote that marriage did not pull me out of the grave—no one can be our savior but THE Savior–but it did give me a companion inside the grave. Sitting with that sentence exposed how much truth it held. Standing side by side had felt safer than standing alone, but was also a counterfeit to the emotional and spiritual intimacy marriage entails. Familiarity had felt like safety. The semblance of stability had felt like rest. Sitting showed me the difference between being accompanied and being held, without accusing what had been necessary at the time or casting blame on him or me. Data is neutral until we attach emotion to it. The bird's-eye experience did not ask me to assign emotion; it only asked me to take note during observation.

None of this required new information to process and feel. It required attention and intention. To swoop into my body at specific points in my memories and pay attention to my body where stress from previous trauma was held. Then, convince myself it was finally safe to process what I wanted to forget and to feel what I didn't want to feel.

Sitting after I was called forth from the grave allowed me to notice how quickly I scanned for collapse. How often I converted feeling into action. How easily faith became responsibility. How standing ready for battle had become procedural—something I did without asking whether it was still required. I would learn how to stand in the armor of God, recognizing which battles I'd been called to fight and which were His alone. A different kind of standing. However, here, I was learning that not all of life was a fight. And that the hypervigilance trauma had taught me came at the expense of peace and joy. My brain had been rewired for protection instead of connection, but trauma would not have the final say.

The calling did not ask me to relive these moments. It asked me to listen to what trauma had trained me to expect. I had learned that love required vigilance. That truth required timing. That faith required endurance. That rest was earned, not received.

But, what if...and in the moment, it was a big *if*, my entire way of being was based on faulty wiring. The answer to rewire my brain back to its factory default setting: to connection rather than protection, was simple in theory and very complex in execution.

Sitting did not correct those lessons all at once. It named them. This was not healing...yet. This was orientation. I was no longer asking why it had happened to me. Although I had yet to learn that not every event in my past was a cosmic or personal attack. This isn't Heaven, and we're all flawed humans. I was learning to ask what posture those experiences had formed—and whether I was willing to keep living from a place of trauma or shift to living from a place of healing.

The journey from trauma to healing is quite a trek. It can be long. We are rewarded with a beautiful vista at the top of the mountains we conquer. However, when compounded trauma occurs, the mountain peak often gives way to the next valley, and we can feel the Grave beckon back to us from the depths of the trough. Life in general has an ebb and flow, marked by seasons of triumph and testing. But when we are making the journey as someone with unresolved trauma, the typical seasons of highs and lows life gives everyone are made difficult by the baggage we've yet to process. The compounded effect can bring discouragement and leave one feeling like they have mental whiplash. It can exhaust the most hearty of sojourners who smile and pretend they are not traversing this life with the weight of the world on their shoulders.

The calling did not demand answers, rationalization, or justification. It simply asked me to observe and take note from a place of calm rather than urgency. It asked me to sit long enough to hear the questions being asked behind the glib responses I had mastered for socially polite spaces. And for the first time, I stayed in the stillness. I sat. I did not stand and brace for impact. I did not flinch.

Much like in my life and death moment post-operatively when I was fifteen, here, I stayed in the place of peace God had created for me. From this bird's-eye perch, I watched the trauma happen to my body as an observer who was not yet asked to feel the pain. Here in this space, for the first time, I was able to name what had happened to me. I had been abused.

Abused.

That word was guarded. It brought to mind betraying my family and breaking our code of silence. I gaslit myself trying to point out that I had survived, and being abused implies death…I said as someone newly emerged from the grave. I tried to make myself feel stronger by insisting to myself, I hadn't let her hit me. Thoughts of eight-year-old me dialing "9-1-" fought for the narrative that somehow I had escaped the humiliation of abuse, especially by my parents. Because, if your parents can't love you, who on earth can? *I must be unlovable.* Hands over my ears, don't think that. Don't say that. But even if the words went unsaid, my little heart had already believed it to be true.

Parents. Siblings. School Bullies. School Counselors. They'd all confirmed the rendered judgment that somehow I was born unlovable. And I had been living, hoping no one would find out that truth. No more pain. No more abuse.

They'd [my older siblings] been abused, not me. In talking to my oldest brother, who had experienced more physical forms of abuse than the psychological torture she favored for me when physical abuse was no longer an option, we realized it does no good to compare which type of abuse is worse. It wasn't a club either of us wanted to be accepted into or a badge we wanted to wear.

The carefully constructed facade of a model family was crumbling with each acknowledgment of truth. The choice to reconnect with that trauma, carrying this knowledge, was enough to make me want to stay in a state of dissociation.

I had found Jesus to be my safe haven in the storm. His people were still a crapshoot.

"He got up, rebuked the wind, and said to the sea, 'Silence! Be Still!' The wind ceased, and there was a great calm."
— (Mark 4:39)

CHAPTER 11

Disrupted Identity

"See what an incredible quality of love the Father has shown to us, that we would [be permitted to] be named and called and counted the children of God! And so we are! For this reason, the world does not know us, because it did not know Him." — (1 John 3:1 AMP)

Listening did not bring relief.

It brought disruption.

Once I stopped standing reflexively and stopped translating every internal signal into action, I began to notice how much of my identity had been built around necessity. Not calling. Not desire. Not vision. Not passion. Necessity.

I had become the responsible one because someone had to be.

Responsibility was not a personality trait. It was a role assigned early and reinforced often. I was praised for my emotional maturity and poise from an early age in school. I was so helpful and strong, and yet I felt parentified. It meant anticipating needs before they were spoken. It meant managing emotional weather so storms did not escalate. It meant reading rooms, reading people, and reading silence as often, or more, than I read stories.

Listening exposed how fluent I was in this language. Listening did not make me feel safer. It made me feel exposed.

Responsibility was not something I chose. It settled on me early and stayed because it worked. It meant anticipating emotional shifts before they erupted. It meant managing volatility so it did not spill over. It meant, without instruction, understanding that stability mattered more than truth and that silence mattered more than relief. This form of responsibility is often mislabeled. The world is conditioned to view responsibility as a tangible obligation. The responsibility I held was to hold the line and walk the wall to keep the emotional storms at bay. Not to be too much or too little as to *cause* the black clouds to gather.

Listening revealed how deeply I had internalized this role.

I had learned to manage adults' emotions long before I had words for my own. I knew how to read a room before I entered it. I knew how to soften my presence when tension rose. I knew when to disappear and when to perform, so things wouldn't escalate. I learned that being observant was safer than being expressive, that compliance preserved order, and that naming reality did not guarantee protection from harm.

These were not lessons I remembered learning. They were lessons my body had memorized, forged in the firestorms.

Listening did not just replay the moments where chaos went unaddressed, or harm went unnamed. It allowed me to finally see what those moments had required of me. I had been expected to continue as if nothing had happened. To function while repair was avoided. To move forward, while adults reset systems without addressing the underlying damage.

Standing had been praised. Endurance had been spiritualized. Silence had been mistaken for maturity. The result: I had confused responsibility with identity, and I felt responsible for everything.

Standing had not only kept me alive—it had given me a role that explained my place in the world. If I were responsible, I belonged. If I was useful, I was safe. If I held things together, I would not be abandoned.

Listening threatened this logic.

As the noise quieted, I began to see how procedural my life had become. How often I responded automatically to expectations. How rarely I paused to ask whether something was actually mine to carry. Standing had become efficient—predictable, reliable, reflexive.

Efficiency had once been a strength. Listening revealed it as a survival adaptation that had lost its ability to turn itself off.

A cataclysmic collision with the Holy Spirit fast-tracked my progress in this phase of the calling. I remember not knowing who I was. I had no idea what I stood for and was easily swayed by an influential opinion. Having begged God for wisdom when my daughter was born, God was being faithful to give it to me; I just didn't know how the process worked.

The most pivotal moment in my spiritual growth snuck up on me. I felt compelled to attend a soul-healing retreat where some Spiritual Giants who had been sowing into me were leading. I drove forty-five minutes with my very pregnant friend for what I thought would be a fun weekend.

As we drove, I had recurring thoughts about the name "Ruth." I had never experienced anything like that before. I kept it to myself, just trying not to be "weird". We pulled up, and the name was almost like an intrusive thought. Still, I was excited about what I thought the weekend held.

Walking up to the registration table, I waited for my turn, only for the woman with a beaming smile to say, "Hi, I'm Ruth. What's your name?" Something inside of me was like nope, nope, nope. Rather than say my name, I ran to the bathroom, feeling suddenly very queasy and disoriented. I had my first panic attack. I tried to convince anyone who would listen that I needed to leave.

One of my friends looked at me, still in the bathroom, and said, "You are saying you'd like to take our pregnant friend's keys and leave her out here so you can go home." Yes. I'm absolutely saying that. But, to be fair, I would have taken anyone's keys at that point, not just hers. What I didn't know then but soon learned was that the panic at Ruth was probably due to the first crack in the walls I had spent a lifetime erecting for "safety" beginning to crumble.

Part of the process was taking a personal inventory. One weekend wasn't enough for all the resentment, hurts, and hangups I had amassed, but it was a start. Filling it out was emotional, exhausting, and deeply fulfilling. This wasn't just the bird's-eye view as an observer. This was like being slammed back into my dying body as an "invitation" to feel. Just acknowledging it to myself and giving the hurt names, dates, and a voice started to undo the vise grip in my chest in some ways; in others, it began to tighten.

Wounded inner children long to be heard, even by our adult selves, so this was sacred work that I didn't even know the depths of at the time. These were inner children to whom I hadn't formally been introduced.

We work so hard to push the unlovable and humiliating parts of our story down into the depths of our souls and guard them under chains and padlocks. We put up "Do Not Enter" and "Beware" signs that keep even us out. Monsters grow in the dark and shrink in the light, but acknowledging the truth and allowing ourselves to feel the feelings we've been avoiding can be epically hard and painful.

Ruth approached me on the second day. She was a longtime friend of the woman who would become my mentor and was also a psychotherapist. These prayer warriors who were leading this weekend had created the soul-healing ministry to travel to the war-torn regions of Uganda and South Sudan, where my first mentor was working. Ruth said that while this weekend retreat didn't have any one-on-one spiritual prayer sessions planned, she felt led by the Lord to offer me the opportunity to have one if I was willing.

I can't really convey what I was feeling, but my spirit was definitely willing, though my mind and body were much more reluctant. We went to a quiet, makeshift place backstage with another person who operated as the scribe. There was nothing special about the place, no special music, words, or anything. That's the great thing about our Emmanuel, God with us; He is accessible and available anywhere. This humble space provided a place for me to encounter Him. I was already regularly attending Bible study and even leading a group, but this space was different than anything I had known.

He Changed My Name

"...and I will give [her] a white stone with a new name engraved on the stone which no one knows except the one who receives it." — *(Revelation 2:17)*

Much like when the friends of the paralytic who couldn't get to Jesus on his own were brought through the roof (Mark 2:3-5), intercessors brought me before the throne to be healed, or at least jumpstart the process. I had no idea two hours had passed while I was in the grips of intercession. I've been in a lot of prayer rooms and sacred spaces since this moment. All I know for sure is that we were standing on holy ground.

I spoke of a lot that had happened to me. Halfway through the session, Ruth asked if I was ready to forgive my mother. Uh, no. No, thank you.

I don't think she was expecting that. She knew what I didn't, that unforgiveness presents a huge barrier to being led by and hearing from God and poisons the one who holds on to its bitter seeds. In the process of transitioning from the grave, God needed to uproot the seeds of bitterness and then replant seeds of life and hope as I was being grafted into His vine.

Jesus was really clear about forgiving. Not just once but endlessly (which isn't the same as restoration or reconciliation) (Matthew 18:21-35; Luke 17:3-4). Ruth also knew that to follow Christ is to forgive people who aren't sorry for our own sake, because the measure we use to forgive others will be used on us (Matthew 6:12, 6:14-15; Mark 11:25). This was an unconditional step in understanding my true identity.

She asked what it would take to forgive my mother. I had no clue. After the surgery when I was fifteen, I had started saying, "I hate you", the same way most children would say, "I love you". Part of me felt unheard at that moment in the session, because, and I know I only shared an hour's worth of trauma, but also...were you listening? Her kindness told me she had been. So, we sat in silence; I had been learning to sit in such stillness. And then she said, "Would you like to ask God to help you forgive your mother?" Sure. I could do that. Let Him be responsible for the outcomes. If He wants me to forgive her, then He would have to make that possible.

I said, "Lord, if you want to, help me forgive my mother." I was no longer emotionally or spiritually there in that room. I didn't have to try to tell God all I had been through. He had been there too. And in a weird but absolute way, I now knew He was in all of the lonely and traumatic moments. I had a vision of Jesus' arm (just the arm was visible) outstretched on a cross beam. I began naming, completely unplanned, all of the things my mother had done to me. Each time I named something, I saw the nail being driven into His wrist. Not only could I see it, but I could also hear it audibly as if it were happening right in front of me. I don't know how much of the two-plus hours I spent naming her sins. All I know is that in God's infinite mercy, it was like an onion, and only a certain number of layers were peeled off that day.

When I had run out of things to recount and name, there was a pause. When I was sure there was nothing else in that moment, I saw the cross lifted up, fully visible and...empty. It is finished. I then heard the Lord say to me, "I have changed your name. You are now called One Who Loves the Lord." I don't really remember, but I don't think Ruth or the scribe audibly heard that, but they knew it all the same. I was probably saying it aloud as it was said to me. When I opened my eyes, I wasn't the only one crying. From the prayer for wisdom whispered over Jessica's newborn head to the breaking of generational curses when Sarah Faith was born, God had been leading me here—to the moment He revealed my own true name and identity in Him.

A New Identity

"Immediately Jesus reached out His hand, caught hold of him, and said to him, 'You of little faith, why did you doubt?'" — (Matthew 14:31)

It felt a little like the quiet that follows a storm. This reminded me of the calm that follows a storm, as I grew up. It was different, for sure, but after an emotionally charged moment, there was always an emptiness and a feeling of not quite knowing what to do next. This felt a little like that, only that this time good things had happened, but in some ways, as I recounted my wounds, it felt like I was experiencing the trauma anew.

Either way, I needed time and space to just be, without talking to anyone. I retreated to my room, which probably wasn't the best idea because the enemy followed me, trying to take back the ground I gained.

When strongholds break, it's an internal struggle over who will regain control. I had never heard of anyone having such an experience. I thought of all the people who had disbelieved me in my life. I thought, what if I just *wanted* God to appear and talk to me, and it was really my own psyche? Which, in some respects, may have been easier to process, but I knew down deep where only truth lives that it was real. What I've learned is that battles for identities are often like that. When we realign ourselves with God and who He intended us to be, a mental and spiritual battle of epic proportions ensues.

In the hours that followed, I almost talked myself out of believing the reality and felt both mad and sheepish about the whole thing. I couldn't very well skip the evening session. It was a celebration complete with a bonfire, where (little did I know at the time) we would burn our inventories as a symbol that the work was done. I attended the celebration, but I was pretty standoffish. I made a test of sorts for God; if what happened was real, then a certain song would play. This was an obscure song. Not popular and rarely played, but I had always liked it. I don't know what made me remember it, but it was called I Will Change Your Name.

Sitting at the table by myself, I looked at the program for the evening. There was a playlist, and I was embarrassed at how much I still hoped that song would be on it – it wasn't. I thought I was being silly, but it still felt like rejection, burning afresh.

I opened my Bible and acted deeply in prayer for myself. The international sign for leave me alone. After a bit, I recognized a few chords of a song that was obscure, not popular, and rarely played. "I shall change your name; you will no longer be called Wounded, Outcast, Lonely, or Afraid. I will change your name. Your new name shall be Confidence, Joyfulness, Overcoming One, Faithfulness, Friend of God, One Who Seeks My Face."

As soon as they started playing the song, the tears began falling silently and unbidden. I opened my eyes and saw what would become my life verse. It may have been my blurry eyes filled with tears, but where we usually read "Lazarus", I saw my own name.

"They came, not only because of Jesus, but also to see Melissa, whom He raised from the dead." — (John 12:9b).

That moment was a milestone of epic proportions. There was no going back to the grave, even in the moments I wanted to. It no longer felt the same, and the grave clothes no longer fit just right. Sometimes I stepped tentatively with one foot back in the tomb, but the light of being called forth shone too brightly to retreat.

At this time, I began to notice how often I chose stability over truth—not out of dishonesty, but out of training. I had learned early that truth could destabilize systems that depended on silence. That naming reality did not always result in safety. That sometimes the cost of truth was simply too high.

Here, listening allowed me to see the choices I and others had made without shame. They had not been failures of character. There had been evidence of formation, and I had to acknowledge the vulnerability and unempowered state of my childhood, where the foundation was laid. Formation that taught me the unspoken rules: keep the system intact, absorb the cost quietly, and do not require anyone else to change.

Faith had wrapped itself around this identity seamlessly, attempting to squeeze out the lies and embrace the truth. In *The Grave*, faith had been endurance. I showed up. I did not walk away. I kept going. I believed that faithfulness meant remaining upright—bearing weight without complaint, trusting that perseverance itself was holy. God was constant. Scripture was familiar. My theology held.

But listening revealed something more precise. My concept of refuge had remained theoretical. I trusted God with outcomes, but not with pace. I trusted Him with direction, but not with stillness. I trusted Him enough to survive—but not enough to stop managing myself–and not enough to thrive.

Endurance had replaced refuge. This realization did not arrive as correction. It arrived as grief.

Grief for the child who learned to stand too early.
Grief for the adolescent who learned to manage systems rather than be protected by them.
Grief for the adult who built a life around meeting needs rather than being known.

Listening stripped away the role slowly, but relentlessly.

Without constant responsiveness, I felt unmoored. Without a sense of responsibility to anchor me, I felt unsure of my place. There were moments when I missed the clarity that crisis provided. At least in survival mode, expectations were clear. Needs were obvious. The role was defined.

Listening dismantled that clarity.

For instance, when I sat in a wheelchair with failed surgeries and skin grafts, or when crawling through my non-ADA accessible house, it exposed how often my worth had been tied to usefulness. How belonging had been secured through competence. How presence had been conditional on performance. When those measures were removed, I did not immediately feel free.

I felt unnecessary.

Listening asked questions I had avoided by staying busy:

- Who are you when responsibility is not required?

- What do you believe when endurance is no longer demanded?
- How do you relate to God when faith is not measured by how much you can carry?

This was not a crisis of belief. It was a crisis of identity.

The Calling did not ask me to abandon responsibility. It asked me to examine whether responsibility had become my primary way of belonging in the world. Whether I had learned to secure safety by being indispensable. Whether I had mistaken overfunctioning for maturity and silence for wisdom.

Standing had once been the right response. This state of listening and forced stillness, revealed when it was no longer sufficient.

What unsettled me most was not the loss of the role, but the absence of a replacement. Listening did not offer a new identity to step into. It created space—an unstructured, unfamiliar space where certainty dissolved and the old measures of worth no longer applied. This was deeply uncomfortable.

There were days when I wanted the role back. Days when I longed for the familiar weight of responsibility, the relief of being needed, the clarity of knowing what was expected of me. Now, women from the church cleaned my house, cooked my meals, grocery shopped, and helped with my children, all with zero expectation of reciprocity. Listening did not indulge my need to be needed. It held the space long enough for something truer to emerge.

Slowly, I began to notice how much energy had been spent maintaining equilibrium—anticipating reactions, managing outcomes, preventing collapse. I realized how often I had absorbed tension so that others wouldn't have to feel it. How many decisions had been shaped by what would keep things calm rather than what was true?

Listening did not condemn these patterns. It exposed what it had cost me.

Responsibility without rest had narrowed my life. Silence without safety had fragmented my sense of self. Faith without refuge had become effort disguised as devotion.

The Calling did not resolve this tension quickly. It intensified it.

Listening did not bring relief. It brought honesty. It asked me to sit with the fact that the survival self I had relied on could not carry me into the next season. That the posture that had kept me alive could not make me whole. My wounded body was now a physical manifestation of this truth.

This chapter did not end with clarity. It ended with surrender. Not surrender as collapse, but surrender as release—the slow loosening of a role I had mistaken for myself. For the first time, I didn't rush to alleviate the discomfort. I did not manage the fallout. I did not take responsibility for restoring equilibrium.

I stayed. I laid my hopes and dreams...my identity I held...on the altar believing that on Mt. Moriah, the Lord would provide (Genesis 22:14). And staying, though unfamiliar and unsettling, was the first honest response I had made in a long time.

"...yet, not my will, but Yours be done." — (Luke 22:42)

CHAPTER 12

Laura's Love

"Trust in the Lord with all your heart, lean not on your own understanding. In all your ways acknowledge Him, and we will make your path straight." — (Proverbs 3:5-6)

Listening not only disrupted my identity. It exposed the cost of the silence that had protected it.

Silence had never felt neutral to me. It had felt strategic. Necessary. Like standing, it was a posture I learned early and practiced well. Silence kept things from escalating. Silence preserved order. Silence allowed life to move forward without asking questions that did not come with safe answers.

In *The Grave*, I learned how to be quiet in ways that appeared to be mature. In *The Calling*, listening differentiated its counterfeit: silence that costs the user and that hides abuse and dysfunction. The silence found in stillness enables listening rather than just hearing and comes with peace and support.

I had learned that truth was not inherently redemptive in the moment. Truth was made to be weaponized contextually, interpreted by those who knew only opinions. Truth required timing. Truth demanded discernment—not about whether it was right, but about whether it could be survived. I had learned that naming reality did not guarantee protection, repair, or care. Sometimes, it only guaranteed a consequence from a world that preferred the facades that adhered to societal norms.

There is no room for messy there. So I learned that silence could contain the mess, though the cost of that vigilance marked those on the outside looking in.

There had been moments when truth mattered most. Moments when authority paused and waited. Moments when my words could have shifted outcomes. I knew exactly what was being asked of me in those spaces. And I had known, just as clearly, what telling the truth would cost. So, like in my mother's hearing, I didn't.

I lied. Efficiently.

Not dramatically. Not emotionally. Not maliciously. I gave answers that preserved the system. I said just enough to keep things intact and just little enough to avoid fallout. In those moments, silence was not absence—it was participation. A willful act of omission that was the same as lying, as far as my young heart was concerned. It was the final act of responsibility in a system that had taught me my role well. And, I betrayed myself in the process.

I had lived inside a family rule that never needed to be spoken to be enforced: *We do not air dirty laundry.* Silence was not weakness. It was loyalty. It was protection. It was the price of belonging to the dysfunctional group, which I was made to believe, was better than being alone. After all, if you can't make it in your own family, where can you survive? Who will love you if they can't?

Listening revealed how deeply I had internalized that rule. How quickly my body still responded to it. It wasn't just a learned response. It was the default wiring I had been taught, although the factory reset indicated otherwise. I became aware of how often I felt the reflex to minimize, to soften, to manage perception rather than speak plainly. Silence had become a moral posture—one that appeared to be integrity but functioned like erasure.

And I had been praised for it as a child. This didn't translate well to adult spaces. I was accused of being aloof. They didn't know that the "RBF" wasn't forged from apathy or snobbery, but rather years of calculation to create a default mode of not showing emotion.

Listening made something else painfully clear: silence had not only shaped how I spoke, but also how I listened. It had shaped how I asked for help. Or rather, how I didn't.

I had learned that reaching out was risky. Asking for support could destabilize already fragile systems. That isolation was safer than disappointment. That needing something from someone else created vulnerability without guarantee. In *The Grave*, I wrote that *trauma had rewired my brain for protection*. I had learned that the more out of control a situation became, the more I pushed others away, believing the lie that I was safer in isolation.

Listening brought me face to face with that lie. The moment that made it undeniable came during a season when I had every reason to withdraw. Not for the last time, the steady ground on which I thought I was standing gave way, and everything I thought I knew became disoriented.

It's worth repeating that it's the people along the way who make the difference, good and bad. The "good" ones are the gifts we collect along the way. My greatest gift here was the catalyst for change that would facilitate a legacy change. Laura Casper. I had asked her to be my mentor at a transitional moment in her own life. After she had suffered through breast cancer, whose treatment left her needing a double radical mastectomy and open heart surgery, followed closely by Parkinson's that would force her exit from her long-beloved elementary school classroom. She wondered what the next season of her life would bring, just as I was adrift like a ship without a rudder. God knew. He had all of eternity to answer both of our prayers through each other.

In this moment, I was in a manual wheelchair. My body had once again become unreliable after my first freak accident with the shopping cart. I was in a wheelchair or with assistive devices for four years. By this time, Laura had been walking with me for about six years. I had already had my soul-healing moment with Ruth and was sitting at the feet of spiritual giants, a Timothy to their Paul.

But the grave made a concerted effort to pull me all the way back in. My daughter was sick—*eventually diagnosed with Celiac's, but we didn't know that then*. All we knew was that she was vomiting eight to twelve times a day for almost a year and was now in crisis. She was misdiagnosed with a rare disorder that I didn't believe she had (I was right, and the doctors were wrong). I was determined to get her treatment on the right track. I was exhausted, overwhelmed, and beyond my capacity to manage one more variable. I did what silence had trained me to do.

I stopped answering the phone. Isolate. Withdraw. Nothing makes sense. Find safety.

Laura didn't get that memo. Or, knowing her, she did. She had a way of seeing through the fault to the need. She always created space, lent her faith, and provided hope, without being pushy. She had been calling me a few times, and I hadn't answered for a couple of days.

I told myself I was protecting my energy. That I didn't have the bandwidth. That explanation would take more than I could give. Unfortunately, I was at the end of my rope: sitting in a wheelchair in the lobby for a much-needed break while my husband, who was working at the same hospital, was giving me a reprieve in our daughter's room. There were no answers coming for her. I was fighting doctors who had misdiagnosed her (later proven by another team of doctors through blood tests and whose diagnosis provided the cure). I was still mom to a three-year-old, a seven-year-old, and an eleven-year-old. I was spread too thin and not doing much of anything well, it seemed. When the phone rang again, and I answered, my words came out sharp and defensive before I could filter them.

"Can't you take a hint? I don't want to talk to you?"

Silence had always worked before. But Laura did not respond the way silence had trained me to expect. She, a six-foot-tall woman with a crown of gray glory whose demeanor commanded attention but was never loud, said in her sing-song voice, "No, I don't suppose I can. I'll be right there."

She came.

That sentence has stayed with me—not because of its tenderness, but because of its disruption.

Laura did not ask permission. She did not require explanation. She did not negotiate access. She did not punish my withdrawal. She did not disappear. Listening allowed me to understand what that moment actually did.

It did not rescue me. It did not fix my circumstances. It did not undo what silence had already cost me. But it revealed, unmistakably, that silence was not the only language love spoke.

Laura did not treat my withdrawal as rejection. She did not interpret my defensiveness as a boundary she needed to respect in order to maintain presence. She moved toward me without demanding that I be ready, regulated, or agreeable.

Her presence broke something open in me. Her *radical kindness* broke me.

That breaking was not an emotional release. It was recognition.

For the first time, authority did not feel dangerous. Care did not require performance. Presence did not demand explanation. Someone came— not because I asked well, not because I deserved it, not because I managed the interaction correctly—but because they loved me and found *me* worth it. She *wanted* to come and just be present.

Listening helped me see that this was the first time my nervous system had experienced that particular grammar of love. Laura did not undo the years of silence that preceded her. She did not rewrite my past. But she contradicted it.

She showed me that silence had been costly. However, there was an alternative way to move forward. Transformation was possible, and I could be transformed by the renewing of my mind (Romans 12:2). Radical kindness was the catalyst, the spark that lit the flame to ignite sustainable change.

This realization did not immediately make me brave. It made me aware.

Aware of how often I had mistaken isolation for wisdom.
Aware of how often I had spiritualized endurance to avoid vulnerability.
Aware of how many relationships I had kept at arm's length because silence felt safer than being seen.

Listening did not ask me to confront silence aggressively. It asked me to be honest about it.

To notice how quickly my body still defaulted to withdrawal. How reflexively I still managed myself to avoid being a burden. How deeply I still believed that needing something from someone else required justification.

Laura's presence did not correct these patterns. It exposed them.

And in doing so, it created the smallest crack in a system that had once felt airtight.

For the first time, I could imagine that truth might not always come at the cost of connection. That being honest might not always result in abandonment. That silence might not be the highest form of maturity.

Listening did not demand that I speak more. It asked me to examine why I hadn't. It did not demand that I trust myself or others immediately; it simply asked me to observe the path that had led to that conclusion. Listening did not ask me to embrace my inherent worth as an image bearer of God, simply worthy of love; it just asked me to feel for a moment what it was like to be unconditionally loved, not in prayer or by God, but with His hands and feet wrapped around me by her.

This chapter does not end with a resolution.

It ends with a question that would not leave me alone:

If silence was not the only option—
If presence could exist without explanation—
If someone could come without being summoned—

What else might be possible if I stopped protecting myself from the very thing I needed?

The Calling did not ask me to answer that question yet. It asked me to sit with it.

And for the first time, instead of retreating into silence, instead of managing the discomfort, instead of telling myself I was safer alone—I stayed...with her. We sat together in stillness, and everything else felt just a little bit more manageable.

"Little children (believers, dear ones), let us not love [merely in theory] with word or with tongue [giving lip service to compassion], but in action and in truth [in practice and in sincerity, because practical acts of love are more than words]."
— (1 John 3:18 AMP)

Learning to Walk

"He will teach us His ways, so that we may walk in His paths." — Isaiah 2:3

After the old logic of endurance began to fracture—after silence lost its neutrality—I noticed that returning to the way things had always been no longer felt automatic. It felt chosen. Deliberate. Like stepping back into a posture my body had already begun to resist.

For most of my life, survival had required proof.

Proof that I could endure.
Proof that I could adapt.
Proof that I could keep going even when stopping would have made sense.

Listening did not remove that instinct. It exposed it.

It would be an interesting metaphor, but rather than a metaphor, it was my inner life mirrored in full expression to my physical recovery. Like a baby learning the way of the world from crawling to walking and creating neuropathways as mental roadmap for life, so too was I being born again into a real spirituality (though I had long had a relationship with God), a new paradigm shift on healthy, functional relationships (vertical, inward, and outward), a type of learning to walk again.

I had been told I would not walk again without assistance. That my right leg—Achilles severed at the ankle, surgeries failed, skin grafts failures stacked—would not cooperate the way it once had. Doctors offered amputation as the logical solution. It would be cleaner. More efficient. Easier to manage.

Endurance heard that as a challenge.

I had learned a new way of doing many things, but I did not yet know how to rest well. I had endured several bouts of forced bed rest, but even then, my mind and spirit remained in overdrive. What I knew was how to persist. The thought of quitting in trials was a foreign concept. Life had been harder than easy. I didn't know we could just quit. So I learned to walk again, the only way I knew how—through repetition, discipline, and a kind of faith that looked suspiciously like stubbornness.

The first three physical therapists gave up on the notion that I would ever walk again without assistance and discharged me for having unrealistic goals and failure to progress. The fourth, she believed. I dropped my children off at school and then worked physical therapy like a full-time job. I showed up when my body resisted. I stayed upright even when it hurt. For sure, I wanted to quit many times I just didn't know how.

Eventually, I walked. Then I ran a 5K. Then a 10K. Then I summited mountains.

This was a victory. But it certainly complicated what I was learning about rest and listening to my body.

Learning to walk again taught my body that healing was possible—but it also reinforced the idea that healing required effort, vigilance, and constant management. It taught me that progress came from pushing, that strength was proven through endurance, and that stopping was a dangerous thing to do. It was a tangled web in my mind to process how some elements of each extreme are good at the same time.

Actually, the middle ground of tension held between extremes is called balance. Whether from CPTSD or ADHD, or my innate wiring, I often leaned towards all-or-nothing approaches. It seemed that the infant stage of being called out of the grave included the baby steps that allowed for such black-and-white approaches, inherent in extremes. Maturing required a more complex application of when each was appropriate and how to contextualize tools to work together in harmony.

My body learned that it was not permanently broken and that what was broken could be repaired, or at least healed, so it could still be usable.

That mattered.

Even years later, listening could trace the impact of that knowing. Once the body has experienced recovery, the thought of resignation feels heavier. Once healing has occurred, even imperfectly, hopelessness loses its innocence. This would be foundational to all that was to come in body, mind, and spirit. I learned I could make it through one more day. I learned to keep believing regardless of who believes with you. I learned that I could do far more than I could have imagined because of the power within me.

Being believed once does not make you whole. It makes you aware.

The next reset in my life came geographically. I didn't want to leave Kansas City, though Laura was moving to Florida. Darin wanted somewhere more rural. I had no idea what that meant, or that there was a separate rule book for rural living that no one would give me.

It seemed appropriate, given all I had learned and healed from in the last decade, that a new start where no one knew I'd been in a wheelchair for four years, or the version of me before significant integrated healing took place, to begin a new chapter of the journey in a new place. New land. New routines. New surroundings. Space to breathe. I told myself this was wisdom—that sometimes the healthiest thing you can do is step away from what keeps you braced for impact.

At first, I thought it would help cement what I'd learned, but it was largely disorienting.

The pace slowed. The edges softened. The constant background noise quieted just enough to notice how loud my internal world still was. I was trying to no longer react to immediate threats, but my body did not know that. It kept scanning. Kept anticipating. Kept standing. And I found a whole new host of threats lying in wait, which did nothing to convince my inner child that we could stand down and stay still in silence.

Listening revealed the truth I had avoided: changing geography does not automatically change formation, and though I trusted God, His people were still a crapshoot.

Arkansas gave me beauty, but it did not give me rest. The silence there was different, but it was still silence. I could hear myself more clearly, but I still didn't know how to respond differently to what I heard.

Still, something shifted.

The distance made patterns visible. It showed me how much of my life had been organized around staying upright rather than staying present. It revealed how often I had mistaken calm for safety and distance for healing.

Being believed once does not mean you stop returning to old strategies. It means you begin to recognize them. It was a lonely time without my support system from Kansas City and those who didn't understand why we would move in the first place.

Our first year there was tumultuous. A storm was brewing, searching for a weakness in the wall to breach the inner sanctum. Some old spiritual battles were waged with new faces to carry out the assignments, and some new diabolical strategies were unleashed. It felt like being under siege.

When Sarah got sick in sixth grade, the fear arrived immediately and completely. Not dramatic fear—focused fear. Clinical. Alert. The kind that mobilizes every system in the body at once. My attention narrowed. My instincts sharpened. My world reorganized itself around one objective: keep her safe.

I knew how to do this.

I monitored symptoms. I tracked patterns. I asked the right questions. I pushed for answers. I absorbed the uncertainty without letting it spill outward. I did not collapse. But this time brought significant moments of panic.

I still stood...now, shakily.

Listening would later reveal that this was a transitional phase, a time to sit in stillness.

Sarah's illness did not teach me anything new. It activated something old. The belief that love meant vigilance. That responsibility required constant alertness. That if I stayed on my feet long enough, if I managed the variables well enough, I could outrun harm. But somehow, it still found us.

Sarah had a near syncope episode during basketball practice. One of Darin's colleagues, a cardiologist, ran an EKG and found that she had a long QT interval. That got us sent to the Children's hospital for a very thorough battery of tests. The pediatric cardiologist was unable to reproduce the long QT wave. After extensive stress testing, the heart was declared that of an athlete. However, they also ran several lung tests, including thorough pulmonary function tests. Through their comprehensive work-up, this cardiologist told us that Sarah had interstitial lung disease, and their best guess was that she would have five years to live or need a lung transplant.

Whoosh. All of the air, all of the energy, all of my everything left me. I was struggling to find air for my own lungs to breathe.

In that season, silence returned—not as withdrawal, but as containment. I did not speak the fear out loud because I did not yet know how to do that without increasing it. I carried it quietly. Efficiently. I functioned. But I also broke. I had gotten through my crisis of faith with six back-to-back miscarriages...four from carrying her "womb mates." How could this little fighter, who had made it through all of the tenuous circumstances to live, have all of that taken away now?

I couldn't unknow all I had learned. I had already taken steps out of the grave that was desperately calling me back to lie down. Circumstances from every angle were bombarding us. Threatening our very existence, daring us to keep going forward when we'd found people and life in general to be so cruel. It was a war within. It was a spiritual battle. It was a physical decisiveness that allowed me to keep getting up and moving forward.

"Eloi, Eloi, lama sabachtani" "My God, my God, why have you forsaken me?" (Mark 15:34). If Jesus, who never sinned, could cry out from the cross, I could cry out in my anguish and suffering too.

I did. He's bigger. The rest of that thought process is surrendering to the fact that my ways are not His ways and my thoughts are not His thoughts. He's God, and I'm not. Surrender.

National Jewish Health in Denver took Sarah's case, though it was a months-long wait to get in. Those months were hell. She and I went to

Denver for two and a half weeks, where she turned twelve. She had a thorough battery of tests, finding she had very small lungs and a narrowing of her throat due to a laryngeal obstruction when her body was put under stress. BUT she would not need a lung transplant. The outcome was better than we could have asked or imagined, but walking through the stress of what-ifs and having to surrender again and again throughout the daily walk was transformative in itself.

Even after Sarah recovered, my body did not stand down. The alarm stayed on. The tension lingered. The readiness to respond never fully powered down. I had protected her—but I had also reinforced the belief that safety depended on my vigilance. This was reinforced when, after returning, Darin had back surgery, was out of work for 10 months, and then traveled for work, leaving me alone in a foreign place where allyship was hard to find.

The physical circumstances matched my spiritual landscape. I was out of the grave, and the grave clothes no longer fit right. But I was not fully immersed in the other side of calling. Yes, I had been called forth. My name was changed. But I had yet to find my Calling.

In a moment of desperation, I called Laura. Of course, *she came*. She and Bob stayed for two weeks and helped me find stillness through the disorientation of standing, vigilance, and exhaustion.

Learning to walk again had shown me my body could recover.
Sarah's illness and Darin's surgery showed me how quickly I still defaulted to control. But I had already learned it is just an illusion.

Listening connected those dots.

It showed me that endurance had become my primary language of love. That silence had become my primary strategy for managing fear. That faith had often been practiced as an effort rather than a refuge.

None of these realizations felt condemning.

They felt clarifying.

Listening did not ask me to stop loving fiercely.
It asked me to notice how much fear had been embedded in my devotion.

It makes returning to them conscious.

After the injury, after the move, after Sarah's illness, something in me could no longer pretend that standing was neutral. The cost was visible now. The tension was audible. The exhaustion was undeniable.

The Calling was not asking me to abandon responsibility, but rather to be curious about what it had for me.

It was asking me to question whether responsibility had become the only way I knew how to be faithful.

This chapter does not end with a resolution.

It ends with recognition.

Recognition that healing had already begun, even when I did not have language for it. That my body had learned, in fragments, that safety was possible. That once learned, even briefly, silence and endurance could no longer carry the same authority.

Being believed once—by my own recovery, by the truth revealed in distance, by the fierce clarity of loving my child—had changed something irreversible.

I could still stand. But I could no longer pretend that standing was the same as living.

Listening did not rush to fix that tension. It asked me to stay with it.

And for the first time, instead of managing the fear, instead of outrunning the ache, instead of returning to silence as a strategy—

I was patient in stillness. I channeled the energy of standing into outreach. I began to pour into others while I listened and waited on God.

"But those who wait for the Lord [who expect, look for, and hope in Him] will gain new strength and renew their power; they will lift up their wings [and rise up close to God] like eagles [rising toward the sun]; they will run and not become weary, they will walk and not grow tired." — (Isaiah 40:31 AMP)

CHAPTER 14

Speak Lord, I'm Listening

"The Lord came, stood there, and called as before, 'Samuel, Samuel!' Samuel responded, 'Speak, for your servant is listening.'" — 1 Samuel 3:10

The Calling did not arrive as an urgency. That was the first way I knew it was different.

For most of my life, anything that mattered arrived with pressure attached. Responsibility announced itself loudly. Needs demanded a response. Purpose felt inseparable from motion. If something was good, it needed to be done quickly. If something was right, it needed to be carried immediately before something bad could happen. Trauma led me to believe that something bad would always happen.

Listening had already begun to dismantle that logic.

By the time I could hear the Calling clearly, urgency no longer felt like obedience. It felt like residue—leftover energy from a nervous system that had learned to equate movement with safety and stillness with risk. The Calling did not ask me to move faster; it asked me to move intentionally.

It asked me to embrace the dichotomy of staying in stillness even as I move. I didn't yet know this was the abiding lifestyle.

That distinction mattered more than I could have articulated at the time.

By this time, pouring into others had become a way of life. It actually began while still lying in the grave. Wounded warriors recognize other wounded hearts, and I often felt called to respond to them as I wish others had responded to me. This was especially true regarding children, the most unempowered demographic.

I was on the Board of the River Run for Orphans in Kansas City, part of the Center for Orphan Justice. Actually, outreach started organically during my summer in the inner city when I was nineteen. I'd always been involved in women's and children's ministry, whether formally or informally. This carried over to Arkansas, where I was on one of the hospital's outreach Boards working on scholarships for young women, where I worked to free indentured servants, worked at a center for recovering addicts, and also in the times I introduced some of the most vulnerable souls to Jesus as they waited to be taken from their home by DHS.

You see the calling, and my Calling didn't ask me to divest myself of all I'd been through or to waste those experiences. They asked me to reframe them through the lens of integrated healing so that I could serve as a guide to those whose paths included suffering... many times different from my own in circumstance... but, in emotional honesty, they were similar.

In line with that part of my character, I've been on many youth trips as the female leader, often at the eleventh hour. So, when I was asked at the last minute to be the female leader on the church's youth group trip to camp, especially one my children were on, I said yes.

Part of the need to stay standing, braced for attack, is the unknown each day brings. Trauma usually comes on an ordinary day when you least expect it. The extraordinary days always begin as ordinary, good, or bad. No one wakes up knowing that this is the day they'll get the call that brings them to their knees or promotes them. While this is true for everyone, those whose brains are rewired by trauma are hypervigilant, stay braced for attack to try to at least respond quickly enough to deflect the arrows away from vital parts of life.

This time, the extraordinary moment triggered a seismic shift that no amount of hypervigilance could have predicted. While we were at camp, the leaders were separated from the campers for leadership training. This was a large venue that afforded considerable anonymity.

During the worship portion of the leadership training, I felt as though the Lord was whispering to me, *"Let go of what you're holding on to so you can receive what I have for you."* I, presuming to know what the Lord means, began letting go of distractions from home so I could better pour into the students with us. Clearly on the wrong track, the Lord was more emphatic.

The director of the camp interrupted worship at the mic and said, "I feel the Lord is saying to someone in this room: *You've got to let go of what you're holding onto to receive what I have for you.*" I was simultaneously thunderstruck and heard from God: *You're going back to school.*

Wait...what? You mean in seven years, when my youngest graduates from high school? I learned promotion in one's Calling rarely comes at a conveniently planned time.

When the invitation to return to seminary surfaced, it did not feel dramatic or heroic. My spirit sensed the calm movement as a natural progression, one I had never considered before. It did not come with a sense of destiny or validation. My mind and body did not receive this new venture calmly. They craved the confirmation of destiny or a strong sense of external validation that my inner self refused to yield.

Naturally, I went to Laura and Bob's. My two youngest daughters were there already, so it was scheduled. However, God had a more significant timing in mind for this trip to affect His divine plan. I borrowed their faith in my ability and confirmation of my Calling, and they held me accountable to applying.

I had believed deeply for years. I had endured faithfully. I had trusted God without reservation. And yet, much of my faith had been practiced without refuge. I knew how to show up. I did not know how to rest. I knew how to serve. I did not know how to lead myself and others well or independently as a guide. Although I was born with a gift of leadership, it was honed in a dysfunctional battle that eventually yielded to the spiritual battlefield. Now, it was time to refine those skills for furthering the Kingdom, though I could not have articulated why I was there at the onset. I added an extra focus on leadership to the standard seminary curriculum.

Listening had exposed that gap.

Seminary did not appear as a place to fix myself or prove anything. It appeared as a place where the questions that had formed my life might finally be allowed to exist without being rushed toward resolution.

That alone made it feel dangerous to the pathways in my brain still influenced by trauma.

Earlier in my life, I would have approached education as another form of standing—another way to remain competent, another way to justify my voice, another way to turn suffering into usefulness. The impulse to do that still lived in me. But not here. Not at seminary. Seminary required introspection, challenge, and surrender.

Returning to seminary required a different posture than I had ever brought to learning before. I was not there to win arguments or collect answers. I was there to listen—deeply, slowly, and honestly—to theology that did not bypass the body, to Scripture that did not require silence, and to questions that did not threaten belonging.

Here, faith required wrestling. There were no pat answers and rote dogma. I was unaware of the existence of seminaries prior to my admission. I found out most didn't graduate women so that narrowed the choices considerably. Gordon-Conwell Theological Seminary has always graduated women, and it is an interdenominational seminary. It is hard to imagine a better format. Here, we acknowledged the gray areas and grappled with our personal tenets of faith, considering how they fit alongside a God who refused to be contained within human constructs.

Faith was something I was allowed to inhabit as much as it inhabited me.

That changed everything.

Seminary became a place where my lived experience was not an inconvenience or a liability. It was not something to overcome in order to be credible. It was treated as data—meaningful, complex, and worthy of attention. I could name suffering without being accused of doubt. I could ask questions without being perceived as a threat.

Listening had prepared me for that space. Being heard and learning to truly listen were essential aspects of wrestling.

It had stripped away the belief that obedience required certainty. It had dismantled the reflex to manage perception. It had loosened the grip of the survival identity that once told me my value lay in how much I could carry. And let the realization that I was never meant to carry the load begin to infiltrate my mind before it traveled the long distance to my heart.

His yoke is easy. His burden is light. (Matthew 11:30)

The Calling did not ask me to become someone new. It asked me to become integrated.

That integration did not arrive all at once. It formed gradually, through hours of reading, reflection, prayer, and dialogue that did not demand resolution. More sitting in stillness, contemplating, asking for wisdom...listening. I began to see how faulty theology from my childhood had shaped my nervous system without my consent—and how healthy theology could also contribute to its healing through abiding prayer.

Scripture began to sound different.

Not louder. Not more authoritative. More embodied.

I noticed how often I had read the Bible as instruction rather than invitation. How frequently I had turned faith into a discipline of endurance rather than a place of refuge. Seminary did not dismantle my faith.

It deepened it. I already walked with a limp, literally and figuratively. My name had already been changed years earlier. I had been called to come forth out of the grave, and I came. Not a linear walk. Not a run. However, I consistently came forth in the calling. Now, here, I was discerning my Calling.

It would take years to recognize, but the seeds of Calling were planted there. Dr. Rodney Cooper was another person who became a gift along the way. He was my professor and my advisor. Many people enter seminary knowing exactly what their next step will be. Me? I had no idea, except for obedience.

In my first class with Dr. Cooper, during my first semester at seminary, a course was offered that examined the soul. I didn't know it would come, but looking back, I can see how, in both seminary and psychology studies, it is a necessary component, akin to the "physician heal thyself" type of axiom. His assignment to create our timeline to share with the class made me wonder how much to share. I was fine sharing my trauma, but I had a lifetime of experience that said people found it to be too much in large chunks. He had me talk to him privately to share a bit about my concern. He listened, then pronounced, "Yours is a story that must be told."

No. No, thank you. I heard that, similarly, after my accident, but still – no. I don't mind talking to people or in front of crowds. Writing is a gift, but I do not want to tell *my* story.

The Calling continued after seminary, but it did not escalate into ambition. It clarified into responsibility—not the old kind that required vigilance and overfunctioning, but a quieter responsibility to steward what I was beginning to understand.

I continued my postgraduate education not because I needed more credentials, but because I was compelled*...called... to create space for others to transform and become legacy changers, as I had.*

I had seen too much to turn away. I had watched people suffer under systems that rewarded performative motions and punished honesty. I had watched leaders burn out while calling it faithfulness. I had watched trauma masquerade as character flaws and silence be mistaken for maturity.

Listening had shown me the cost of that confusion. And Calling began to whisper: *there's a better way.*

The introspective practice continued as I pursued an intensive, year-long advanced graduate certificate program at Fielding University. Here, I applied the stillness and peace I had learned for myself, and now was the time to develop the platform to hold such a space for others. This is similar to the group that brought their lame friend through the roof for

Jesus to heal, because he could not reach him on his own (Mark 2). Coaching and leadership coaching became intercession, taking physical form.

My own life ebbed and flowed through the healing process. Trauma still came unbidden. Those who should have been trustworthy proved themselves to be untrustworthy. Roles can be meaningless, words can be cheap; always believe actions.

Then, the call came way too soon. Laura was dying, imminently. With the world still shut down due to COVID, the call came anyway. No, she didn't have COVID, but heart disease and Parkinson's didn't care about shutdowns. We drove through the night.

She didn't look like she was dying. As a matter of fact, I chuckle thinking back to the first words out of her mouth when she saw me, "I am so sorry." She wasn't saying that to be polite about the long, frantic trip. She was saying that to the little girl in me, who was about to say goodbye to the mama who had reparented her inner child. To unconditional love with real arms that hugged. To the one who always *came*. On her last day on earth, Laura wasn't thinking of herself; she still prioritized others, even *me*.

Very late that night, she ran into the arms of her friend, Lord, and Savior, Jesus, while we sang Amazing Grace at her bedside. We wept, for us. She rejoiced at being home and made whole.

There was an emptiness there. This wasn't stillness, really. This was grief. A grief that can still, these years later, sneak into my heart like an ache that never is far away. She was the gift that taught me there were gifts along the way and how to be a gift to others.

I felt lost at sea. My anchor was tied to a failsafe, a guide through life's storms who always pointed me back to God. Well done, good and faithful servant, receive your reward (Matthew 25:23). I will try desperately to be the Timothy that rises to your Paul.

"But because God was so gracious, and so very generous, here I am. And I'm not about to let his grace go to waste. Haven't I worked hard trying to do more than any of the others? Even then, my work didn't amount to all that much. It was God giving me the work to do, God giving me energy to do it. So whether you heard it from me or from those others, it's all the same: We spoke God's truth and you entrusted your lives."
— (1 Corinthians 15:10-11)

CHAPTER 15

Reframing and Expanding

> *"We are pressured in every way [hedged in], but not crushed; perplexed [unsure of finding a way out], but not driven to despair, hunted down and persecuted, but not deserted [to stand alone]; struck down, but never destroyed;"* — *2 Corinthians 4:8-9*

The Calling had always been there. I just needed enough stillness to hear it, and enough trust to surrender the need to control it.

The voice I had longed to hear did not arrive the way I once imagined.

It did not interrupt my life with thunder or certainty. It did not dictate next steps or resolve the questions that had followed me for years. It did not explain my story back to me in a way that made everything suddenly make sense.

It taught me how to listen.

For most of my life, I believed that hearing God meant receiving instruction—clear, unmistakable direction that removed doubt and made obedience obvious. I had been trained, implicitly and explicitly, to associate faithfulness with clarity and certainty with trust. When clarity was absent, I assumed I had missed something. When certainty felt elusive, I wondered whether I was failing spiritually.

Listening began to dismantle that framework.

By the time I reached this season, I had learned that not all voices deserve equal authority. Some are loud because they are anxious. Some are persistent because they are familiar. Some feel urgent because they are rooted in fear rather than wisdom. All of them could appear in my internal dialogue. Listening taught me that discernment is not about volume—it is about alignment and purposeful attunement.

That realization altered my understanding of the voice I was seeking.

There were moments when this new way of listening felt less like peace and more like exposure. I would notice my body pause where it used to rush, a tightening in my chest when urgency did not immediately resolve into action. My hands would hover, unsure of what to do next, as if waiting for instructions that no longer came. Sitting with that hesitation felt risky. I had learned to trust movement more than stillness, decisiveness more than discernment. Reframing required me to stay present in the space between impulse and response, and that space was not yet comfortable.

The retreat marked a threshold. Not because everything changed immediately, but because something irreversible began there. The moment of naming—of seeing my own name in Scripture—did not give me answers. It gave me orientation. It told me who I was before telling me what to do.

That mattered more than I knew at the time.

After that, life did not simplify. It expanded. Listening did not narrow my focus; it deepened it. I began to notice how often I had interpreted my experiences through a lens shaped by threat rather than truth. How easily I defaulted to worst-case assumptions. How frequently I framed my story around survival rather than meaning.

Listening did not erase those habits. Listening became a running dialogue–an abiding prayer–It gave me the ability to question habits, memories, thought loops, and agreements. Reframing emerged as the discipline that arose from that questioning.

At first, reframing felt artificial—like forcing a different interpretation onto experiences that still carried weight. I worried that reframing might be a form of denial or spiritual bypassing, a way of dressing pain up in prettier language. But listening showed me something different.

Reframing was not about minimizing what had happened; it was about locating it and letting it process accurately. It was about being in a space where I felt safe enough to finally feel and process without ascribing guilt, shame, or blame to myself for having needs or wants. It was acknowledging the truth of what happened, going back to the versions of myself who experienced those events, then walking alongside them to thank them for getting us through and to let them know they could finally rest. This memory no longer required anyone to stand guard. The adult me was ready to be in charge of that area.

This process leaves room for the focus to shift from the negative aspects of trauma, without minimizing them, and to log any positives that may emerge, even if they're only lessons or fresh insights. It separates out memories from an overwhelming conglomerate into individual moments, allowing for a microscopic view of all the players in the scene. It may not excuse their actions, but it can facilitate understanding and help establish healthy boundaries in our minds and in real life.

I began to understand that many of the interpretations I continued to make in life were viewed through a template that trauma had created. They were conclusions drawn by a nervous system trained to anticipate danger. They had once been protective. They were no longer reliable.

I can now recognize emerging patterns and be empowered to choose my response rather than react. Inherent in that is recognizing the people I had allowed into my inner circle and restructuring who belonged in what circle to effect peace. Boundaries could be maintained without hypervigilance on the wall, but it took work, a different kind of work.

This insight followed me into my doctoral work.

But first, there was COVID.

As I was engaged in the process of relocating for vocational ministry, COVID hit out of nowhere on an ordinary day. I was traveling. Then I was on bed rest.

Again.

Hyperbaric oxygen. Infusion therapy. Refusing to go to the hospital for admission. Inability to sleep for days that turned into weeks that turned into months. I felt betrayed by my body. I didn't ask, "Why me?" Rather, I already knew, "Why not me?" I was resigned. I was isolated. My brain didn't cooperate with my goals. I developed trigeminal neuralgia from COVID that entered through the nasal ganglia. I developed a desire to exit the pain in my body...again. The grave beckoned me back, further in than ever before. I felt it at times as a physical grip rather than a spiritual one.

I knew I *could* go on. Everyone told me how strong I was. "You got this!" Yes. I could. But this time, I just didn't know if I wanted to. Darin would say to me, "Just one more day. You can make it just one more day." And, I did.

I went to the end of myself in this forced stillness. I let God carry the load and prayed for my children, whose mother was forced into bed rest and isolation one more time as their father worked long hours.

In the quiet when I couldn't read. Couldn't focus. I maintained my inner garden, where truth resides, and His name is Jesus (John 14:6). This was a time of great reframing. To move forward meant choosing joy actively from within my own prison. Different than Paul's in

Philippians, but still the same effect. I was empowered to choose my mindset and my focus. Letting go of what was out of my control and embracing what was within my control. Arising from this battle was the final testament to proving oneself as a spiritual warrior in combat. I was emerging resembling the spiritual giants at whose feet I used to sit. I had sat with Laura long enough to let her voice remain as an internal sage. Now, she was guiding me still and pointing me back to God.

I had already been accepted to my doctoral program in psychology. The commitment and something on the calendar that persisted is probably what kept me going, as work has largely been suspended during COVID, mine and the world's.

Psychology did not arrive as a replacement for faith. It arrived as a companion. A way of naming what the body had always known but had never been given language to express. Research did not distance me from lived experience. It honored it.

Education did not detract from my story; it brought clarity to it. It balanced all I had experienced, aligning with my faith, and now, education was lending its balance.

This season unfolded slowly, over months and then years, as the world recalibrated after COVID and I entered my doctoral work. Time no longer moved in clean chapters. Days blurred together, punctuated by study, uncertainty, and the quiet discipline of showing up again and again without the reassurance of immediate outcome. There were mornings I questioned whether this path made sense, evenings when fatigue whispered that I had misread the invitation entirely. Listening did not remove those doubts. It taught me how to hold them without letting them decide for me.

Somewhere along that path, I was given another quiet gift. My professor, who later became my dissertation chair, advisor, and voluntary mentor,

Dr. Jay Colker, embodied the same kind of steady presence I had learned to recognize as trustworthy. He did not rush the process or impose certainty where it didn't belong. He asked thoughtful questions. He made space for integration rather than performance. Working with him reinforced what listening had already taught me—that formation cannot be hurried, and that wisdom often arrives through patience rather than pressure. His mentorship was not loud or dramatic. It was consistent. And that consistency mattered.

What surprised me most during this season was how little internal resistance I felt. Earlier decisions in my life had been accompanied by anxiety, pressure, and the fear of getting it wrong. This decision felt different. Not easy—but settled.

I was not trying to outrun my past or redeem it. I was no longer even trying to understand it. I was researching how to integrate all that I had learned about leadership, coaching, and psychology to equip and empower agents of change to alter their own outcomes and change the cultures wherever they held influence.

Post-COVID, the world was collectively disoriented. Systems I had trusted proved fragile. Institutions I believed were stable revealed fault lines. The pace of life had shifted, but the expectations remained the same. Academia, in particular, carried its own kind of urgency—quiet, relentless, and rarely questioned.

I entered my Ph.D. program with a different posture than I would have earlier in my life.

I was not there to prove myself. I was not there to outrun my past or redeem it through achievement. I was there because listening had taught me that language matters—especially when it comes to human behavior, leadership, and systems shaped by trauma.

What I was learning academically mirrored what I had learned spiritually.

Cognitive reframing is not about pretending circumstances are different from what they are. It is about examining the meaning assigned to those circumstances and asking whether that meaning is accurate, adaptive, or true. In psychology, reframing allows individuals to step out of automatic interpretations and consider alternative explanations that are less catastrophic and more grounded in reality. Facts may not change, but understanding can declaw the monster that keeps triggering.

Listening had been doing that work in me long before I had words for it.

My studies provided me with the language to describe patterns I had lived with for decades. I began to see how beliefs formed under threat can persist long after the threat has passed. How leadership styles often reflect unresolved fear. How systems reward overfunctioning and punish vulnerability while calling it excellence. *And, I knew we could be better individually and collectively.*

Reframing allowed me to name those patterns without being owned by them. It also changed how I understood hearing God.

The voice I longed to hear was not one that removed effort or struggle; it was one that acknowledged it. It was the voice that taught me how to pause between stimulus and response. How to notice my first interpretation and ask whether it was rooted in fear or truth. How to distinguish conviction from anxiety and wisdom from urgency.

Listening trained me to ask different questions.

Not catastrophizing: *What is the worst-case scenario?*
But: *What is actually happening here?*

Not: *How do I prevent loss?*
But: *What is being invited?*

Not: *How do I stay safe?*
But: *How do I stay aligned and attuned with God?*

This was not passive listening. It required discipline. It required restraint. It required humility to admit that my first interpretation was not always the most accurate. And to effect that outcome, I had to cultivate an abiding lifestyle that was aligned and attuned with the Shepherd, because His sheep know His voice (John 10:27).

Reframing did not make the work easier. In some ways, it made it heavier. When fear surfaced, I could no longer dismiss it as truth. When old narratives reappeared, I could no longer obey them without question. That awareness carried responsibility. It meant I had to choose my response consciously rather than reflexively, and conscious choice requires energy. There were days when reverting to old interpretations felt tempting simply because they were familiar. Listening asked me to remain awake where I once could coast.

During the uncertainty of the post-COVID world, that discipline became essential.

There were moments when the old narratives resurfaced—stories about scarcity, instability, and the need to stay vigilant. Listening did not prevent those thoughts from arising. It gave me the ability to reframe them in real time.

Fear said: *This is unsafe. You're not enough.*
Listening asked: *Is it unfamiliar, or is it actually dangerous? Aren't you created in the image of God?*

Anxiety said: *You are behind. Your children are missing out. Trauma is around the corner.*
Listening asked: *Behind whose timeline? Isn't God the sustainer when you cannot be? But what if it isn't?*

Self-doubt said: *You don't belong here. You don't have it figured out as they do.*

Listening asked: *What evidence supports that claim? Who has what figured out?*

Reframing did not make the work easier. It made it truer.

I began to recognize that hearing God's voice often sounded like clarity rather than command. Like alignment rather than instruction. Like a steady sense of "this aligns and is true" rather than a dramatic sense of "this is urgent."

That realization changed how I approached leadership, research, and even faith.

I stopped looking for signs that would absolve me of responsibility. I stopped waiting for certainty before acting. I learned to trust the quiet integration that emerged when listening, reflection, and action aligned.

The voice I longed to hear was not external; it was internal. It was cultivated in the inner garden.

It was the voice that emerged when fear was no longer allowed to narrate my story unchecked. When urgency was questioned rather than obeyed. When meaning was assigned intentionally rather than reactively.

This did not mean I stopped listening to others. It meant I became more discerning about which voices shaped my interpretations. It meant I could receive feedback without collapsing or feeling the need to defend myself. It meant I could engage complexity without rushing toward resolution. The culmination of my experience, my faith, and my education was shaping the space where stillness did not produce discomfort. Quiet moments didn't need to be filled. We can wait for answers to emerge at the perfect time. These coaching experiences did not detract from or minimize the leadership and strategic gifts that were still applied decisively when consulting with organizations. This was a balance that moved seamlessly within me, my relationships, the space I held for individuals, and the guidance I provided the collective.

In many ways, my doctoral work became an extension of my spiritual formation.

Both required patience.
Both demanded humility.
Both taught me to sit with ambiguity without panic.

Listening had taught me that reframing is not an intellectual exercise—it is a spiritual practice.

It is the practice of choosing truth over habit. Of allowing new meaning to emerge where old interpretations once ruled. Recognizing that the story you tell yourself about your life shapes how you live within it. And I began to apply this cumulatively in listening circles for those whose voices had long been suppressed. Guiding others to find their voice and learn to amplify it in a way that produces change rather than just noise to be heard became foundational as my Calling took shape.

Listening had already dismantled the belief that calling required urgency. It had revealed how much of my earlier obedience had been driven by fear rather than alignment. This time, saying yes did not feel like standing taller or carrying more.

It felt like consent. Consent to learn without self-erasure. Consent to ask questions without punishment. Consent to let understanding take time while embracing the paradox that an abiding lifestyle provides alignment and attunement to remain decisive.

There were moments when I realized how different this posture was from those in earlier seasons. In the past, I would have taken on this work as proof that suffering had been worthwhile. Another attempt to make pain productive.

This time, I did not need to justify my story. I needed to be faithful to it.

The Calling did not promise impact or visibility. It did not assure me that the work would be recognized or celebrated. It did not offer a platform or a plan.

It simply asked me to remain. And in the remaining, urgency was replaced with authority.

Authority not as control, but as integration and expertise. As the quiet confidence that comes from living inside alignment rather than obligation. From knowing that what you are doing matches your Calling.

This chapter does not end with arrival.

It ends with reception.

I did not seize the Calling.
I did not chase it.
I did not prove myself worthy of it.

I received it.

And for the first time, obedience did not require me to be vigilant, impressive, or endlessly capable. It asked me to be present, attentive, and honest—to let my education serve integration rather than ambition, and my voice serve presence rather than performance.

The voice I longed to hear did not tell me what my future would look like. It taught me how to interpret the present. That, I have learned, is the greater gift.

This chapter does not end with answers.

It ends with a renewed posture.

A posture of listening that reframes rather than reacts–that questions fear-based narratives–that trusts alignment over urgency–that understands hearing God's voice as an ongoing practice rather than a single moment of revelation.

Even now, I feel the pull of urgency in my body before I recognize it in my thoughts. A quickening breath. A subtle leaning forward. Listening has taught me to notice those signals without automatically obeying them. Sometimes that means sitting quietly with discomfort longer than I would like. Sometimes it means choosing alignment over efficiency, truth over speed. The voice I longed to hear did not remove uncertainty from my life. It taught me how to live faithfully inside it.

The voice I longed to hear is no longer something for which I am waiting. It is something I have learned to recognize that has always been speaking to me from within.

And that has changed everything.

"Then he was told, 'Go stand on the mountain at attention before God. God will pass by.' A hurricane wind ripped through the mountains and shattered the rocks before God, but God wasn't to be found in the wind; after the wind an earthquake, but God wasn't in the earthquake; and after the earthquake fire, but God wasn't in the fire; and after the fire a gentle and quiet whisper. When Elijah heard the quiet voice..."
— (1 Kings 19:12-13a)

CHAPTER 16

The Trap Door

> *"And to the angel (divine messenger) of the church in Philadelphia write: These are the words of the Holy One, the True One, He who has the key [to the house] of David, He who opens and no one will [be able to] shut, and He who shuts and no one opens: 'I know your deeds. See, I have set before you an open door which no one is able to shut, for you have a little power, and have kept My word, and have not renounced or denied My name.'" — Revelation 3:7-8 AMP*

I had been here before. So many times before.

That was the first thought that surfaced as I lay flat on my back, staring at a ceiling I did not expect to be studying so closely again. The bed was familiar territory. Immobility was not new. Interruption had become a recurring theme in my life, one I thought I had learned to navigate with some measure of grace.

And yet, this time was different.

I had plenty of time to recount the trauma of the last year. My niece, yes, that niece, has her own timeline like an erratic EKG. However, there are no words to say or write about the moment you find out your baby is going to die. It wasn't until he was a year and a half that they had a name for the developmental delays. Sandhoff disease. One word can suck all the air out of the room until no one feels they have space to breathe. And naming it did nothing to stop the relentless tidal wave of consuming grief that was to come.

Though this was different than my own trauma, I had experience with moments when the steady ground you think you're standing on gives way, and you free-fall into an abyss, figuratively, of course. So, I did what Laura had done for me in such moments. I came. Initially, my visits became more frequent. Then we all came together to celebrate a traditional holiday. We were there to be together–we were there to form a complete circle around him and his family. Then, the four and a half hour drive just seemed too far to breach the chasm of space between houses. The last time I visited, they asked me to stay. So, I stayed.

I looked at the grave they were in–the trauma over the years and new and ongoing grief that held this beautiful family. I saw all of the misery and discomfort that would not relent and only keep growing as the end grew near, and then still there would be waves of grief anew. I hugged the grieving parents, tried to bring some normalcy to the other two children, and then I realized how glad I was that I had learned to sit in stillness. Because his room, a hospice nursery, became sacred ground. As I rocked and sang to a dying baby for months, I remained aligned and attuned to the only One I knew who could bear such a load. Especially when none of it made sense.

I'll never forget the sunrise on the day he took his last breath. We stood vigil for as long as it took–too long. Then comes the devastation after the storm as the survivors survey the damage and wonder how the rest of the world is still turning.

I'm reminded of the times in my life I had cried out: *My God, my God, why have you forsaken me?* Or when people said *You're so strong! You'll get through this.* To which my inner response was *I know I can; I'm just not sure I want to.* And so now, I already knew that there are no words. Those who have learned to sit in the stillness come alongside those in the grave. No words are necessary or even helpful, just presence.

I stayed six weeks after he passed. Then, as they tried to find some semblance of normalcy, I decided to also attempt to merge back into life after trauma. On the four-and-a-half-hour drive home, the coach and psychologist in me was proud of the healthy, functional plans I had made. I pulled into the garage, but before I could set foot into the house, I fell through a trap door. Literally.

The fall itself was sudden. There was a storm shelter built into the garage floor that must have been unlocked and not relocked while I was away. I took one step with my left leg, which used to be my good leg, and it slid forward, stuck on the sliding door. With nothing for my right leg to grab onto, it continued down, and I with it until I landed with a thud!

I went down.

Metal. Concrete. Impact.

As I lay there, injured and unable to move, I noticed what *didn't* happen.

I didn't panic.
I didn't rage.
I didn't bargain.

Though I know this to be a trauma response and my brain to have been unwilling to accept its fate quite yet, I was more concerned about my computer and water cup. Until I tried to move. A quick inventory had me believing I had broken my left hip. I couldn't move it well, and it was excruciatingly painful when I did. My daughter, halfway through her doctorate in physical therapy, was the only other one there. She wanted to run... so did I... but we both stayed.

She wanted me to call an ambulance. I said call your dad. His calm voice broke the tension, and he said, *Take the ambulance.* They didn't know, just like the Achilles tendon accident, trauma wouldn't let me. Trauma said *Don't cause a scene. Don't be seen. Don't be heard. It isn't safe to feel. You're too vulnerable.*

I army-crawled out of the pit while Sarah held my leg in extension by sheer grit and adrenaline alone. I couldn't sit up. I couldn't roll over. It took a while, but we improvised to get me facedown, diagonally in the back of my Jeep Wrangler, and I myself remained dissociatively calm as I told Sarah she needed to do the same while driving me to the emergency room.

Fast forward to lying in my own bed, I had plenty of time to analyze why I, who we now know had a back broken in two places, a pelvic avulsion fracture, and tore all of the hamstrings in my left leg...that used to be my good leg, let trauma still call the shots as my default. Disappointing for sure.

I skipped past denial faster than I expected. I mostly skipped anger. I even moved through disappointment more quickly than felt reasonable. Not because those emotions were unavailable to me, but because I had been here before and never found them helpful. Bed rest with miscarriages. Bed rest with complicated pregnancies. Bed rest after another freak accident that had left me relearning how to walk for years. Bed rest with COVID. Bed rest with too many accidents, surgeries, and illnesses to list.

The bed is familiar territory for someone whose body has repeatedly demanded surrender.

But this time, surrender felt different. It was too egregious to be ordinary. This one incident, along with the cumulative total, was the last straw, and I could no longer compartmentalize it.

My body still hurt. There were sharp reminders in the simplest movements—reaching, shifting, breathing too deeply—that this was not an abstract interruption. Pain made its own demands, and there were moments when frustration flared before faith had time to respond, as I couldn't use crutches, roll over, or sit up because of my back. I noticed the familiar temptation to interpret suffering as failure, to wonder what I had misread or delayed. Listening did not erase those thoughts. It steadied me long enough to let them pass without granting them authority or agreement.

The trap door was not just an injury. It was not simply another chapter in a long history of physical limitation and recovery. It was a stripping away of my remaining distractions. A removal of my last reliable coping mechanisms. A forced confrontation with stillness that I could no longer outmaneuver with resilience or productivity.

I was flat on my back.

Again.

And this time, I could hear it. Not audibly. Not dramatically. But unmistakably.

The question I uttered did not come as an accusation or an explanation. It came as an invitation:

*What would You like me to do with **this**?*

That question had surfaced before in my life, but never with such clarity. In earlier seasons, I had asked it anxiously, hoping for instructions that would restore motion and control. This time, I asked it without urgency. Without bargaining. Without needing the answer to arrive quickly.

For the first time, I was not trying to get out of the situation. I was listening inside it. And what I heard was not a new assignment. It was an old one that had been reuttered.

Write your story.

Not as therapy. Not as proof. Not as testimony dressed up to inspire.

Write it as obedience. Write it as a testament.

I did not feel inspired. I did not feel confident. I did not feel ready. I felt called forth out of the grave and Called to this work.

That distinction mattered.

There were moments when I felt the pull of old strategies—the urge to plan my way out, to assign meaning quickly, to make the interruption productive so it would justify its cost. That reflex was familiar and persuasive. It promised control and resolution. Listening asked me to notice it without obeying it. I was learning that not every disruption required interpretation, and not every delay needed to be redeemed.

As soon as I could sit up enough to reach my computer—still immobilized, still limited, still stripped of every familiar way of being useful—I began to write. Not because I had something polished to offer, but because I had finally learned the difference between urgency and alignment.

This was not the first time I had been told to write. It was, however, the first time I obeyed without resistance, excuse, or trepidation.

Earlier in my life, writing would have been another way to stand—another way to make meaning out of pain, another attempt to redeem suffering through usefulness. This time, writing came from stillness. From receptivity. From the quiet authority that listening had cultivated.

I was no longer writing *to* become something. I was writing *from* who I had become.

The words came slowly at first, then steadily. I wrote conversations with God. I wrote questions without answers. I wrote what it felt like to live inside a body shaped by trauma and a faith that had matured through restraint rather than resolution.

I did not know where the writing would lead. I did not need to. What surprised me was what happened next.

Doors opened that I did not knock on. Doors opened that I didn't even know *to* knock on.

My name was mentioned in rooms I had never been in. Conversations began that I did not initiate. Invitations arrived that I had not positioned myself to receive. Speaking opportunities surfaced not because I marketed myself, but because someone had read something and recognized themselves in it.

The same was true professionally.

Business ideas took shape organically, not as strategies but as responses. God brought friends and business partners for the journey, not for competition, but for collaboration. Needs were named in rooms I did not know existed. People reached out with questions that mirrored my own from years earlier. Opportunities emerged that aligned with the work I had already been doing internally.

I did not chase any of it.

That was new.

In earlier seasons, momentum would have triggered a sense of urgency. Opportunity would have activated the old reflex to prove, to perform, to capitalize. This time, I noticed something else instead.

Peace.

Not the absence of effort, but the absence of panic. I could say yes without grasping. I could say no without fear. I could move without losing stillness.

The Calling had shifted what I knew about my existence.

It was no longer asking me to prepare. It was asking me to participate.

The trap door had not derailed my life. It had clarified it.

As I look back now, I can see how many times I had been called before—called forth out of the grave, called out of silence, called out of endurance, called out of identities that no longer fit. Each calling out led to something greater, which is ironic, how hard that is to discern at the time. Each calling had required surrender, but this one required something different.

Trust.

Trust that obedience did not require acceleration or having it all figured out.
Trust that alignment would open doors without force.
Trust that my story did not need to be managed in order to matter.

This time, being flat on my back–again–did not feel like regression.

It felt like confirmation.

The grave clothes no longer fit. Even when I tried to put them back on, they felt restrictive and unnecessary. The situation looked familiar, but my approach to it was different. I could still stand. I could still work. I could still lead.

But I no longer believed that standing was the same as thriving, and I had been called to an abundant life.

Writing this story is not the end of the Calling. It was a long-awaited beginning for the second season of my life.

I remember the quiet of those early writing days—no agenda, no audience, no certainty about where the words would lead. Just the soft hum of the house, the weight of the laptop on my legs, and the steady awareness that this was enough for now. I did not need to stand for the words I was writing. I did not need to prove anything. I only needed to stay present to what had been given, trusting that obedience practiced in stillness would carry its own momentum.

Not because it completed anything, but because it released me into availability. Availability to speak when invited, because I had found my voice. Availability to build when aligned, because I was attuned with God and knew my Calling. Availability to witness without striving, because He was in charge of outcomes.

This chapter does not end with arrival. It ends with obedience that feels quiet, grounded, and sustainable.

I had been called before. But this time, I answered.

And that answer changed the shape of everything that followed.

"This is God's Message, the God who made earth, made it livable and lasting, known everywhere as God: 'Call to me and I will answer you. I'll tell you marvelous and wondrous things that you could never figure out on your own.'" — (Jeremiah 33:2-3 MSG)

The Witness

"For you will be a witness to all people [testifying] of what you have seen and heard." — Acts 22:15

CHAPTER 17

Before I Knew What Witness Meant

"You also will testify, because you have been with Me from the beginning." —John 15:27

I did not wake up one day and decide to become a witness.

I did not claim it.
I did not prepare for it.
I did not even recognize that I was a witness at first.

For most of my life, witnessing had been something I *did* without language, without pomp and circumstance, or announcement. It was something that flowed from necessity, proximity, or responsibility. I showed up where there was a need. I offered the only truth I had as a survivor and overcomer. I walked in when the rest of the world walked out, and I stayed when others left, because I knew what it was to be in the silence alone. I absorbed what could not be held elsewhere. I called it service, obedience, leadership, or simply doing what was required–if I called it anything at all.

Somewhere along the way, I realized I had crossed a threshold. I was no longer trying to understand what had happened to me; I was noticing how I now moved through the world because of it. This was not the end of the formation. It was the beginning of witness—not as testimony or explanation, but as perception. The work had already been done quietly.

What remained was learning how to see and navigate the world through a new lens.

I did not yet know that what I was offering was a form of witness.

That realization came much later—only after survival loosened its grip and listening taught me how to see my own life with clarity rather than urgency.

Before that, witnessing happened in fragments.

It happened in hospital rooms and kitchens, in borrowed spaces and late-night conversations, in moments when people were vulnerable enough to tell the truth because someone stayed long enough to hear it. I learned early how to recognize suffering—not because I sought it out, but because it was familiar. Wounded warriors recognize other wounded hearts. I did not need to be taught how to enter those spaces. I had lived in them, and they'd become a part of me.

I witnessed in the inner city when I was nineteen, long before I had the language for what I was seeing or what it was costing me, or that it was costing me at all. I witnessed in women's ministry and children's ministry, formally and informally, because those were the places where power was least protected, and pain was least hidden, though the bearers of it valiantly tried. I witnessed alongside addicts, alongside those being extracted from unsafe homes, alongside women whose stories were interrupted by systems that moved faster than healing. Looking back, Jesus often makes His presence known among groups where there is a systemic imbalance of power.

At the time, I believed this was simply a matter of obedience. It did not feel remarkable. It felt necessary.

But necessity is not the same as formation.

Looking back, I can see how much of that early witnessing was driven by a need for survival. I knew how to stay. I knew how to endure proximity to pain without collapsing. I knew how to hold space because I had learned how to disappear inside it. That kind of witnessing is costly in ways that are not immediately visible. Some wounded warriors witness because they haven't learned to navigate life without chaos. Though their own lives may no longer be marked by immediate trauma, they come alongside others to be near its proximity so they won't have to exit the grave and, thereby, stand down, sit in the stillness, and allow their own trauma to be healed.

I did not yet know how to distinguish between *presence* and *overfunctioning*.

Still, the witness was real.

It happened again in Arkansas, where I found myself drawn into work that mirrored the same pattern—hospital outreach, scholarship efforts, advocacy for young women, quiet ministry among those with the least amplified voice. I did not plan these roles strategically. They arrived organically, often through relationships rather than resumes. I showed up because I was asked. I stayed because it mattered.

I believed this was what faith looked like. And in many ways, it was. But it was not yet whole. What changed was not the work. What changed was me.

Writing this book forced a distance I had never taken before. For the first time, I was not inside the work reacting to need. I have been observing my life long enough to notice what has been happening beneath the surface.

Writing gave me distance, and distance gave me data. My researcher's brain began to engage—not to analyze my life clinically, but to notice what had been happening beneath the surface all along. I wasn't looking for conclusions. I was noticing repetition. Whispers of powerful questions threaded through my thoughts as I wrote.

Throughout my post-graduate studies, my research tendencies were sharpened. Though there were times in writing the arc of my transformation that I was able to grieve for the losses of what was and what never was but should have been. Mostly, though, the years-long work I had done through soul-healing had helped me deal with the events and declaw the monsters. Now, I can observe my story of change as an adult and an expert – more neutrally and with a spirit of curiosity. My researcher's brain—trained to look for patterns rather than isolated moments—and questions began to surface that I had not asked before.

This wasn't an intentional process. I had no objective when I started writing. There was no hidden agenda. I approached it from a place of obedience, when there is nowhere left to run and no strength left to try to anyway. I believe it was this open-handed posture that allowed the major breakthrough. What God wanted to show me had never been fully realized up to that point because it took me not trying to define the space of my story. And my story was something I had protected to the death. This story and my inner children, who resided in it, were why I stood watch on the wall of my heart for so many years.

Mind you, this was all in hindsight. This process wasn't intentional, though I now recommend it. I had played the role of minister, coach, and psychologist to myself many times before. Now, it was only fair that the researcher take her seat at the table to help pull it all together and do what she does best - observe, ask powerful questions, listen, and gather data for analysis. The seminarian answered many questions about the faith journey. The coach and psychologist provided theory that explained thought patterns and behaviors. Still, there were gaps in the literature that could not explain certain phenomena. Among the many questions that emerged, here were some notable ones:

Why did transformation milestones tend to follow certain moments and not others?

Why did some interventions catalyze change while others simply managed crisis?

Why did healing accelerate in environments that felt relationally safe—even when circumstances remained difficult?

I had not been looking for a framework, much less a blueprint. I noticed one anyway.

Across every season of meaningful change—my own and others'—there was a consistent driver that preceded movement: radical kindness.

Not kindness as niceness.

Not kindness as accommodation.

Not kindness as emotional indulgence.

Not every day or even random acts of kindness. The type of kindness that drives sustainable change is radical. Radical kindness arrived as presence without agenda. As staying without fixing. As care that did not demand performance or repayment. It lowered the threat. It restored agency. It created enough safety for truth to emerge without force. It did not depend on or look for reciprocity. It defied social norms. It defied expectation and disoriented those used to judgment. Radical kindness came toward when the rest of the world not only could walk away, but often did, as a socially and clinically sound response, whether it was acceptable or not.

I had seen it again and again.

I had experienced it personally. I had watched it change rooms. I had seen it disrupt systems that relied on fear to maintain control, both internal systems and systemic structures.

But I had never named it.

Witness, I began to realize, was not about the moments when I spoke the loudest or acted the bravest. It was about the moments when something shifted simply because someone stayed regulated enough for another person to breathe. Because radical kindness lends faith, lends breath, lends courage, and lends hope through the practice of seeing, hearing, and valuing someone in ways that allow them to belong–just because they are human.

That realization changed how I understood everything I had done before.

Earlier witnessing had been sincere, faithful, and costly. But it had often been driven by urgency—the quiet belief that if I did not stay, something would fall apart. That belief kept me engaged, but it also kept me on my guard. My presence mattered, but it was tethered to responsibility rather than freedom.

Witness did not arrive as a declaration. It showed up in small, repeatable choices—how I oriented myself when anxiety surfaced, how quickly I questioned catastrophic interpretations, how often I chose presence over withdrawal. This was not a finished state. It was a practice. The training of the mind and spirit is as necessary as training the body. And it required the same attentiveness as healing had, just without the urgency.

This witness was different.

It emerged not from survival, but from integration.

As I wrote, I began to recognize how radical kindness had functioned neurologically, relationally, and spiritually in every true transformation I had witnessed. It created conditions for safety. It integrated what trauma had fragmented. It allowed people to access parts of themselves that had been shut down for protection at the expense of connection.

It did not guarantee outcomes. Of note, it did not insist on anything. It made change possible.

It did not forego boundaries or healthy spaces. It brought order to the chaos through presence and stillness, but allowed the witness to walk away and remain whole without losing themselves. This is an abiding lifestyle that is continually filled by the Source of life from a well that never runs dry.

I could not yet name what I was seeing clearly, but I knew it mattered. Certain responses consistently led to safety. Certain kinds of presence preceded movement. Certain moments, marked by unexpected kindness, altered trajectories without force. I did not yet call this a framework. I only knew that once I could see it, I could not unsee it. So I wrestled with my findings.

This was not a theory I developed in isolation. It was an observation born of lived experience, confirmed through study, and refined through practice. The Integrative Transformation Blueprint™ that would later take shape did not arrive as innovation. It arrived as recognition.

Awareness. Connection. Movement.

These steps could not be invented. They existed, waiting to be recognized and made visible. They were patterns I had seen repeat themselves across contexts—families, organizations, ministries, and inner lives. Each phase required radical kindness to function effectively–toward ourselves and others. Without it, awareness turned into shame, connection turned into codependence, and movement turned into burnout.

Witnessing this pattern reshaped my understanding of what it means to be called forth and Called to something bigger than ourselves.

Earlier callings in my life had asked me to *do*. This calling asked me to *see* and to *be*.

To see how the transformation actually works when it is sustainable. To see how often we mistake pressure for purpose. To see how systems replicate trauma when safety is absent—even in well-intentioned spaces prescribed for healing, but deliver a counterfeit of safety.

Launching **The Sage Hill Project** was not a pivot away from my story. It was a continuation of it—this time with clarity and consent. The social enterprise did not emerge from ambition or strategy. It emerged from the recognition that radical kindness could not remain private once its power was understood.

This couldn't be rushed. It couldn't operate in isolation. Witness had become collective.

Where I once moved instinctively toward pain, now I was building structures that allowed others to move toward healing without losing themselves. The work was no longer dependent on my endurance. It was designed to be shared, regulated, and sustainable.

This distinction matters. I had been a witness before. I had not always been whole.

Earlier witnessing had cost me quietly. This one did not require self-erasure. It did not demand that I outrun my own limits. It flowed from integration rather than obligation. But the process couldn't be rushed. It required precise engineering, waiting for the doors to open, and partnership to appear, as well as the actual Architect to move, so that the structure would remain sound long after my time to dwell in it had passed.

That is how I knew it was different.

The witness described in this section is not a culmination of the book. It is a continuation of a life lived differently. It does not replace earlier seasons of faithfulness. It honors them by showing what they were always pointing toward.

Witness, I have learned, is not about visibility. It is about availability.

Availability to notice patterns without rushing to fix them.
Availability to stay present without absorbing what is not yours to carry.
Availability to let transformation unfold at the pace safety allows.

If you have been a witness long before you had language for it—if you have stayed, served, endured, and wondered why some moments changed everything while others simply drained you—this section is for you.

Not to tell you what to do.

But to name what you may already know.

Sometimes the most powerful witness is not the one that announces itself.

It is the one that becomes visible only after you have been formed again, allowing God to bring order to the chaos, enough to recognize it. This was how The Witness began—not with something to say, but with something to notice.

"Get up and stand on your feet. I have appeared to you for this purpose, to appoint you [to serve] as a minister and as a witness [to testify, with authority]" — (Acts 26:16)

CHAPTER 18

The Blueprint Emerges

> *"[I always pray] that the God of our Lord Jesus Christ, the Father of glory, may grant you a spirit of wisdom and of revelation [that gives you a deep and personal and intimate insight] into the true knowledge of Him [for we know the Father through the Son]. And [I pray] that the eyes of your heart [the very center and core of your being] may be enlightened [flooded with light by the Holy Spirit], so that you will know and cherish the hope [the divine guarantee, the confident expectation] to which He has called you,"*
> *— (Ephesians 1:18-19 AMP)*

Once I learned how to see differently, I couldn't return to the way I had been seeing things before.

This was not a dramatic shift. There was no moment of revelation that reorganized everything at once. What changed was quieter and more persistent: certain patterns began to stand out. Not because I was looking for them, but because they repeated themselves with a consistency that was impossible to ignore.

Writing had slowed my life down enough to notice this. Distance created clarity. Clarity created questions. And questions, when held without urgency, tend to reveal more than pat answers ever did.

I was no longer asking why things had happened the way they did. I was asking what consistently preceded change—and, if possibly discerned, what reliably did not.

The answers surprised me.

Transformation, I began to see, was not catalyzed by intensity or even desire for change. It did not follow insight alone. It was rarely initiated by confrontation, explanation, or even good intentions. Some of the most sincere efforts to help others—or myself—had resulted in very little movement at all.

The comprehensive functions of several types of disordered thinking, such as PTSD, CPTSD, and ADHD, among others, affect the executive center of our brains, the prefrontal cortex. The result is divergent thinking, processing, interpreting, and acting. Basically, in every way we interact with our world.

A deeper physiological deep dive is beyond the scope of this chapter and this book. But the concepts are important when considering why internal and external negatively focused efforts to force change can be frustratingly ineffective and perpetuate the shame and guilt loops through repeated attempts at transformation. The effect of which can exacerbate feelings of being unsafe, perpetuating the cycle of staying stuck, and so on, it continues.

When feeling unsafe or threatened, the amygdala initiates a dysfunctional, exaggerated response that can aggravate the entire integrated system cycle, prompting a decision to fight, flee, freeze, or fawn. This is true, even if the present situation does actually entail such a threat, but has triggered a previous response pathway forged by trauma.

At the same time, certain moments—often unremarkable on the surface— had altered trajectories entirely from this norm. Those moments shared something in common. They were marked by safety. Not safety as comfort, and not safety as avoidance. But the kind of relational and internal safety that allows the nervous system to stand down long enough for truth to surface without force. I had lived through enough cycles of change to recognize that safety was not incidental. It was foundational.

As I reviewed my life—early, middle, and recent seasons alike—I noticed that when change *did* occur, it almost always followed the same sequence. There was awareness, yes. However, awareness alone can often lead to feelings of shame or overwhelm. There were lingering questions not of what, but *how* to facilitate sustainable change. Fear, whether of the actual experience or of experiencing shame – whether real or perceived – or other negative emotions, usually only enables a temporary change. Sustainable change–a transformation–is engaged in spaces where we feel psychological, physical, and spiritual safety.

And, safety was almost always ushered in by radical kindness.

Safety can feel disorienting for those accustomed to the vigilance protection requires. There may even be a tendency, or at least a temptation, to shun safety because the known misery has been normalized, and safety requires learning a new way of being for which we were never given a rulebook.

For this reason, it may be that the first few attempts at radical kindness are shunned by those with disordered thinking, but seeds of change are being planted, even if it is one person sowing the seeds, another who waters them, and another yet who comes at just the right season for the harvest.

Each seed planted through radical kindness offers connection.

In each truly transformational moment, there was connection, but only when that connection did not demand performance or agreement. The sequence of connections is also important. Connections aren't random, nor do they happen randomly. Connections are the factory default setting of our brain, that for which we were made.

To awareness, we attach connection. First, vertical connection. Even secular psychology agrees that we were made to be connected to something far greater and bigger than ourselves. It is part of healthy, functional integration. For me, that is God. The only One proven to be faithful in every season.

This vital connection can be hindered by misguided mystical concepts that misinterpret what it means to cultivate the inner space where this connection is nurtured. This can be from those who have never considered their spiritual domain, and it remains an atrophied "limb", so to speak, within their being. For others, about one-third of people in the United States, church wounds or religious trauma, caused by people who claim to be acting on God's behalf but are only flawed humans like us all, can push those who are divergent or plagued by trauma and/or experience disordered thinking away from that connection.

Nevertheless, this is part of an integrated transformation and a crucial aspect of the beneficial healing and change. Radical kindness that creates safety in these spaces is critical. The good news is that God gave us a blueprint to facilitate this space of connection.

Romans 2:4 is Paul writing to believers, admonishing them who knew and followed God about the type of space they were creating. As a side note, it is interesting to me that Jesus saved His strongest words for those who claimed to follow God while being self-righteous or judgmental. Nevertheless, Paul persists in the emphasis in verses 1-3 that we ought not to judge, which is not the same as foregoing discernment.

Paul is not condemning discernment; he is condemning the hypocrisy of moral superiority. The Greek word literally means we are without excuse, meaning the one who judges is exposed by their own standard. This applies to religious individuals, church leaders, moralists, and anyone who is confident that "I'm not like *them*." The judgment seat is forever occupied by the only One qualified, and they're never taking applications. Divine judgment is truthful, comprehensive, and motive-aware. Human judgment is partial, comparative, and image-based.

So now, we know what not to do. Don't judge. What do we do? There are two foundational verses for this. First, I appreciate that Paul doesn't leave us hanging and goes on to tell us himself in verse 4: "Or do you not know, that it's His kindness, restraint, and patience that leads to repentance..." What is repentance? A change of heart or mind–a transformation.

Kindness, I would offer radical kindness, is the first-mentioned driver of transformation. Why? Because it offers space for others to be seen, heard, and valued, fostering a sense of belonging and safety. It's the Laura Caspers of the world who walk in when everyone else walks out. The people who come, like Laura and my niece, when others can't be bothered. The Sally Shipleys who see through the fault to the need. And all the other people who become the gifts along the way. It is through whom God works for a breakthrough, because He loves us too much to leave us in a state of fear and lacking peace.

To kindness, we add restraint or forbearance of seemingly *deserved* judgment. If there is no strength to destroy, I would argue, there is no need for restraint. That which is weak never needs to be restrained. It is only in strength that we exercise restraint to avoid causing damage. Here, Paul emphasizes the power we have when judging others to cause damage, so we restrain our judgment in favor of kindness.

To kindness and restraint, we add patience. Patience that sees through the fault to the need. That doesn't mean we forgo boundaries or take on others' burdens. Patience looks like Laura Casper when responding to a woman in a wheelchair with a sick child at the end of her rope, who is engaging in antisocial behavior by responding in a way meant to push her away, with resolved kindness and love. It's the Sally Shipleys who look beyond the snarky comments and rude or sullen actions of hurting teenagers to make them feel welcome.

And the hardest part of transformation for some people will be applying this kindness, restraint, and patience to themselves–the second connection is inward. When we have vertical connection that allows us to understand that we are not in control, and that the weight of the world does not actually rest on our shoulders. We then look to repair inward connections.

This connection begins with understanding, from a neutral vantage point, what is within our control and what is not. That we are not what we've done or what was done to us. We are made in the image of God, and we are worthy just as we are. We may be scared to try to transform again, the shame loop still activated from past failed attempts. When we begin to talk to ourselves positively, change is possible, and the life we dream of is on the other side of our fear-based decisions.

The overflow of connecting with God and learning who He created us to be allows us to better connect with others. This description of these three connections is actually the most important acts in which we can engage (I've coined it the epic love triangle), as Jesus emphasizes in Mark 12:30-31. We become equipped and empowered to love others when we love God and ourselves with kindness, restraint, and patience.

These outward connections gain traction, and momentum builds. And then, and only then, was there movement—action that felt sustainable rather than reactive. From this momentum becomes a lifestyle of outreach–a pouring out from a place of wholeness, integration, and healing–from a well that won't run dry. Here, the transformed areas begin to emerge.

This pattern did not appear once. It appeared again and again.

I saw it in my own healing. I saw it in leadership contexts. I saw it in families, organizations, and faith communities. I saw it in places where trauma had narrowed perception and in spaces where kindness had widened it again.

I was not trying to develop a framework. I was watching one reveal itself.

The researcher in me recognized what the lived human in me had experienced long before: systems change when threat decreases. People not only change but also become more productive, creative, and collaborative when safety increases. Meaning emerges when the body no longer needs to defend itself or any version of itself that came before.

That was not ideology. It was observation that gave way to framework.

What struck me most was how often transformation had been attributed to the wrong causes. We praised willpower when regulation was doing the work. We credited discipline when connection had made the effort possible. We celebrated breakthroughs without acknowledging the quiet conditions–stillness– that enabled sustained change.

Once I saw this, I could not unsee it.

I began to notice how often change stalled in environments that emphasized urgency, accountability, or intensity without attending to its safety and connection. I saw how quickly insight was weaponized against people who were not yet resourced to act on it. I recognized how easily spiritual language could be used to pressure movement before the nervous system was ready to comply.

These patterns are not malicious. They are misinformed.

In contrast, when safety is present—when people feel seen without being scrutinized, heard without being dismissed, valued for more than outward expressions, and supported without being controlled—something different happens. Awareness no longer collapsed into shame. Connection did not become dependency. Movement did not require burnout.

Safety created space. Space allowed choice. The choice made transformation not only possible, but also desirable.

This was not abstract for me. I had experienced the opposite too many times. I knew what it felt like to be pushed toward change without being held. To be told the truth without being given the safety to metabolize it. To be invited into movement while still bracing for impact.

Those moments rarely produced sustained growth, even if an outward expression changed temporarily, which only reinforced a sense of failure and shame anew when the white-knuckle grip gave way.

Eventually, aggressive efforts toward change without safety and connection produced compliance, collapse, or quiet withdrawal–not transformation.

In contrast, the moments that changed me—often in ways I didn't recognize until much later—were marked by something else entirely. Someone stayed. Someone slowed the pace. Someone did not demand an explanation or an immediate response. Someone trusted that safety would do what pressure never could.

As I began to see this pattern clearly, it reshaped my understanding of what it means to be a witness. Witness was not the act of convincing someone of the truth. It was the practice of creating conditions where truth could be received. Caring comes first, with no hidden agenda, because our role may be limited to sowing seeds of radical kindness. This is not outcome-oriented, though positive outcomes are achieved; it is a way of life.

This distinction mattered deeply.

It meant that witness was less about what I said and more about how I showed up. Less about argument and more about presence. Less about directing outcomes and more about attending to the process.

The more I examined moments of real transformation—both my own and others'—the more obvious this became. Change followed safety, the way plants follow light. Not because they were forced to, but because the environment allowed them to grow.

I saw this in leadership rooms where performance anxiety that led to perfectionism had been mistaken for excellence. I saw it in families where silence had replaced safety and been labeled as maturity. I saw it in faith communities where legalism and numbers had eclipsed discernment.

And I saw it in myself.

The earlier seasons of my life had been marked by endurance. I could stand, manage, perform, and persist. But standing did not create space. It maintained order.

What changed was not my capacity. It was through my external environment, facilitated by connections, that I enabled an internal transformation.

When safety entered—relationally, physically, spiritually—the same capacity produced different outcomes. I no longer used energy to brace against a threat. That energy became available for learning, connection, and movement.

This was not a moral shift. It was a physiological one.

Trauma narrows perception. Safety widens it. And widened perception allows us to imagine alternatives that were previously invisible.

Once I recognized this, I began to see how often we ask people to change without first addressing what their nervous systems are protecting. We appeal to values without creating safety. We demand accountability without offering connection. And then we blame individuals when systems fail.

The pattern was clear. Transformation follows safety. Not permissiveness. Not avoidance. Not indulgence.

Safety.

The kind that reduces threat without erasing responsibility. The kind that allows truth to surface without punishment. The kind that restores agency rather than replacing it.

This recognition was not flattering.

It challenged many of the ways I had participated in systems that prioritized results over regulation, both internally and externally. It forced me to examine moments where I had mistaken urgency for leadership and pressure for clarity.

Seeing the pattern meant taking responsibility for it. Witness, I was learning, is not a neutral observation. It carries an obligation. But the obligation isn't to change others, it's to create an environment and culture that facilitates transformation.

Once we see what makes change possible, we are accountable for how we facilitate—or withhold—those conditions. This is where the work became personal all over again.

I began to notice how often I moved too quickly, even after my posture had been reshaped by formation. How easily I defaulted to problem-solving rather than presence. How tempting it was to explain rather than stay.

Seeing the pattern did not make me immune to old habits. It made them visible. And visibility changed how I related to them—without triggering my own shame or negative emotions. The data is neutral, and I am equipped and empowered to make the shift back to a state of health and function.

Instead of automatically obeying urgency, I could pause. I could enter other people's emergencies without internalizing them as my own. *This isn't my emergency, it's theirs.* Instead of assuming resistance meant defiance, I could consider being curious about what was making the moment feel unsafe. Instead of pushing toward movement, I could attend to what made movement possible.

Was there awareness? How were connections across the three spheres?

This was not passive. It required restraint. Restraint to not swoop in and rescue, to not want change for someone more than they wanted it for themselves. To sit with them from a place of stillness and, having divested myself of judgment, instead engage in curiosity.

Restraint is not often celebrated. It may not *look* like leadership, but there's no need for restraint without strength. It does not *feel* productive. But restraint, when paired with presence, turned out to be one of the most powerful forces for change I had ever encountered.

As I continued to write, teach, coach, and lead, this pattern followed me everywhere. It appeared in different forms, but the sequence remained remarkably consistent.

Awareness without safety led to shame.
Connection without safety led to dependency.
Movement without safety led to burnout.

But when safety was present, awareness became insight, connection became hopeful resilience, and movement became sustainable-transformation.

I did not arrive at this conclusion through reading theory.

I arrived at it through the accumulation of my life experiences, which allowed me to emerge at the intersection of my personal experience, faith, and education.

Through watching what worked.
Through noticing what failed.
Through paying attention long enough to recognize the difference from a neutral vantage point.

The pattern was not new. I had simply been too busy surviving to see it. Now that I could, it demanded something of me.

Not proclamation.
Not expertise.
Not control.

Witness.

Witness that stayed long enough to create space. Witness that trusted safety to do its quiet work. Witness that resisted the urge to rush outcomes in favor of honoring process.

This was the beginning of something new. Not because the work changed, but because my relationship to it did. Once I could see the pattern, I could not unsee it.

And everything that followed would be shaped by that recognition.

"Therefore, any one of you who judges is without excuse. For when you judge another, you condemn yourself, since you, the

judge, do the same things. We know that God's judgment on those who do such things is based on truth. Do you really think—anyone of you who judges those who do such things yet do the same—that you will escape God's judgment? Or do you despise the riches of His kindness, restraint, and patience, not recognizing that God's kindness is intended to lead you to repentance?"
— (Romans 2:1-4)

CHAPTER 19

The Sage Hill Project

"He has told you, O man, what is good; and what does the Lord require of you except to be just, and to love [and to diligently practice] kindness (compassion), and to walk humbly with your God [setting aside any overblown sense of importance or self-righteousness]?"
— (Micah 6:8 AMP)

Radical kindness did not announce itself when it arrived.

It did not enter rooms with language or intention. It did not come with a plan or an outcome. In most of the moments that mattered, it arrived quietly—often unnoticed—doing its work long before anyone named what had changed or recognized its presence.

I began to recognize it not by its volume, but by its effect.

Something would soften. Breath would return. Movement would become possible again—not forced, not urgent, not performative.

That was how I learned to see it.

In the spaces where transformation took root, no one was being convinced. No one was being corrected. No one was being managed toward an acceptable version of themselves. Instead, someone stayed long enough for another person to stop bracing for impact or abandonment.

Though it was quiet, almost ethereal, radical kindness was often disorienting to those whose brains are wired for protection.

I had seen moments like this long before I understood their significance. They had happened in rooms that felt unremarkable, in conversations that never made it into memory as milestones. At the time, I would have described them as "small kindnesses" or "being there for someone."

I didn't yet know how radical they were.

Radical kindness was not the absence of boundaries. It was the presence of regulation. It did not remove responsibility. It made responsibility bearable. It did not fix pain. It made pain survivable without requiring explanation or speed.

I noticed how often it arrived precisely where pressure had failed.

In places where people had been told what to do but had never been placed in an environment safe enough to carry it out. In environments where insight had been offered repeatedly, without anyone asking whether the mind, body, or spirit could tolerate it. In moments where truth had been spoken clearly but without the conditions required for it to land transformatively.

Pressure demanded movement, which can result in internal or externally expressed aggression or dissociation.
Kindness created space. That space changed everything, but not usually all at once.

I watched people make different choices—not because they were persuaded, but because they were no longer defending themselves. Though there were plenty of case studies to review, the data could also be accessed simply by interacting with people; my own life and those close to me presented as a case study with robust data. I saw how quickly shame lost its grip when someone felt seen without being scrutinized. I saw how courage emerged naturally when fear was not being amplified. Creativity and productivity peered out again from their dormant posts. And something a little more subtle but, frankly, more impactful–Hope.

These shifts were subtle, yet consistent.

Radical kindness did not look like agreement. It did not avoid hard conversations. It did not excuse harmful behavior. What it did was slow the interaction enough for discernment to replace reaction. Honestly, the broker of this space is often someone who has been transformed, and perhaps that is why it is a space not often cultivated...yet.

Someone would pause instead of escalating.
Someone would ask instead of assuming.
Someone would remain present instead of withdrawing.

Those moments did not feel dramatic. They felt like introducing possibilities, and thus, opportunities.

The problem is that trauma and disordered thinking may make a strong play at pushing others away, even when connection is the answer. When people engage in the logical response and walk away, many say, *That'll teach them.* Or *When will they ever learn?* Or *What's wrong with them?* But radical kindness walks in when the rest of the world walks out. It remains intact and observes, engaging from a place of curiosity.

The person engaging in radical kindness may be someone who offers a brief interaction, sowing a seed in a moment. Or, it may be a relationship that took years of deposits before the pressure causes the new seeds of hope to burst forth. The important tension held in the space of transformation is that there is no damage caused to the person holding such space, because they are already connected to the source of their higher power and pouring from a well that won't run dry. Ideally, they have learned to hold space for others while respecting their own boundaries and avoiding a codependent pattern.

As I continued to pay attention, I began to recognize the pattern more clearly. Wherever radical kindness was present, awareness no longer collapsed into shame. People could acknowledge reality without being crushed by it. Connection did not become codependence because no one was being asked to perform or comply to belong. Movement followed organically, at a pace that did not require burnout.

Radical kindness did not rush outcomes. It trusted process. This trust distinguished it from every other approach I had seen. Most systems prioritize results. They measure success by visible change, by speed, by compliance. Radical kindness measured something else entirely: regulation, safety, and capacity.

Where safety increased, capacity followed.

This was not theoretical. I saw it in families where communication shifted, not because everyone agreed, but because they felt safe enough to stay in the room together. I observed it in leadership spaces, where creativity returned once the fear of failure subsided. I observed it in individuals who had been labeled as resistant, suddenly engaging when pressure was removed.

My mind was racing. Once ideas move from being formed to being proven, an excitement builds. I was tempted to run ahead of where God was leading. Which is actually funny, because I was still flat on my broken back and didn't leave the house for months. I wasn't running anywhere.

Free of distractions, I pursued, not just theory, but the heart of God. This was the vision He'd planted in my heart and would bring to fruition through alignment and attunement. I couldn't begin to know how. So, I listened.

I had long been an agent of change. First, my own transformation, then changing a legacy. Followed by creating space for leaders to change culture, whether in their own minds, their families, their teams, or their organizations. However, looking at the implications and enormity of this change, I felt overwhelmed.

His gentle whisper calmed my racing thoughts and reined me back in. Breathe. *Ruach* (the Hebrew word for breath, wind, spirit–it moves, sends, fills, and sustains). When uttered aloud, it mimics our breath, while acknowledging from whence it comes and His Spirit. It anchored me back in the moment and invited me to use the camera lens as a tool here, too.

Transformation begins with one person at a time, but its impact is far-reaching. So, though the vision of what can happen through a movement of radical kindness has global implications, the inertia shifts through one person at a time.

Slow down. Stay focused. Again, I asked the question. *What do you want me to do with this?*

I was writing my story, this story. But, in real time, a new chapter of my life was being written. The vision of integrated transformation, which acknowledged the driver of radical kindness, was an important discovery in my own healing journey and that of others. So the truth was, I knew the *what* I was asking about in the question I had put to God: *what do you want me to do with this?* It wasn't just "write your story." It was write your story to discover a pattern, a blueprint for how you and others are transformed. Then, educate, equip, and empower. A new question emerged: *How do you want me to facilitate this mission?*

The answer was to mobilize radical kindness. The story had to be written. The integrated transformation blueprint had to come to life as a viable process, a reproducible system for change. The immediate answer didn't become clear because this wasn't an individual endeavor.

God put people in my path that I had not known, nor would I likely have known if I hadn't been obedient in writing my story. But as my story was told, my voice was amplified beyond the roles I played, beyond assignments and expectations. As I began to share my findings, doors opened upon which I didn't even know to knock.

The Sage Hill Project was born. A vehicle to mobilize radical kindness. I had been very intrigued by social enterprises when I first began my doctoral studies at Adler. A mission-minded business designed to give back while operating with a sound business strategy that doesn't rely solely on donations, and is intended to solve social problems. As others weighed in on how to go about the business of mobilizing radical kindness–how could there be individual results with mass implication– I knew that all of my prior experiences, not only in my personal life, but also in early education and business, as well as new and old relationships, would be integral to equipping more agents of change.

The change is not forced. It is an invitation.

That invitation does not come in words. It comes through presence— through someone choosing not to escalate, not to withdraw, not to dominate the space. Through someone remaining grounded enough to hold complexity without demanding resolution.

Radical kindness requires strength.

It is not passive. It demands restraint, self-awareness, and the ability to tolerate discomfort without acting out on others. It requires a regulated nervous system, or at least one committed to becoming regulated.

This is why radical kindness cannot be manufactured. It has to be embodied.

I began to see how often we confuse kindness with softness and restraint with weakness. In reality, radical kindness was one of the most demanding postures I had ever practiced. It asked me to manage my own anxiety before addressing anyone else's. It required me to notice my urge to fix, correct, or rescue—and to pause long enough to choose presence instead.

That pause was where everything changed.

In that pause, fear lost momentum.
In that pause, curiosity emerged.
In that pause, choice became possible.

And the gifts along the way had practiced that pause with me.

I saw how often transformation stalled not because people were unwilling, but because they were overwhelmed. When the nervous system is in survival mode, insight feels like a threat. Change feels dangerous. Even love can feel invasive.

Radical kindness recognized this reality and worked with it rather than against it.

It created conditions where people could remain in relationship with themselves while engaging in growth. Where they could take responsibility without drowning in shame. Where they could move forward without abandoning parts of themselves in the process.

This was the difference between compliance and transformation.

Compliance *looks like* change from the outside. Transformation *is* integration from the inside.

I noticed how often radical kindness preceded integration. How it arrived before insight, before action, before language. How it functioned almost invisibly, lowering defenses long enough for something new to take root.

These moments were not always acknowledged. Often, the person offering radical kindness never knew what they had catalyzed. They simply stayed. They listened. They did not leave when things became uncomfortable. They did not require improvement as proof of worth.

That was enough.

As I reflected on these observations, I realized that radical kindness had been shaping my life long before I gave it a name. Through seeds planted, some in my childhood, it has been present in moments where someone saw me beyond my performance. In seasons when I was allowed to rest without justification. In relationships that prioritize safety over outcome. Those moments did not erase pain. They made healing possible.

Now, as someone formed by those experiences, I recognized a responsibility emerging—not to replicate moments, but to protect conditions. To notice where safety was absent and to resist the urge to replace it with urgency. To create environments—relationally, organizationally, spiritually—where people could access their own capacity without being coerced.

This responsibility did not feel heavy. It felt aligned.

Radical kindness is not something to be deployed; it is something to be practiced. There is still an educating, equipping, and empowering process, but it requires buy-in rather than coercion.

Obstacles to this paradigm shift exist in systems that reward urgency, compliance, and aggressive progress in ways that define the norms without making space to intentionally define a culture that prioritizes creativity, productivity, and collaboration, which can only emerge in spaces of safety. This isn't soft; this is power that exists in a pause. This can only become normalized through visibility and practice.

Practice when fear rises.
Practice when patience runs thin.
Practice when outcomes are unclear.

Practice especially when old habits urge control.

I had been a witness long before I understood this. But this witness did not require me to absorb pain or sacrifice myself in order to remain present. It did not ask me to endure endlessly. It did not tether my worth to my usefulness. It flowed from integration.

That difference mattered.

The work ahead would involve naming this pattern more clearly, translating it into structures and systems, and learning how to steward it beyond individual interactions. But before any of that could happen, it had to be lived.

Radical kindness had to remain what it was: a way of being that allowed for transformation to unfold over time. And, so too would The Sage Hill Project.

Not flashy.
Not fast.
Not loud.

Just faithful.

And once I learned to see it, I could not unsee the way it changed everything it touched.

*"The least will become a thousand, the smallest a mighty nation.
I am Yahweh; I will accomplish it quickly in its time."
— (Isaiah 60:22)*

Doors I Didn't Open

> *"You prepare a table before me in the presence of my enemies; You anointed and refreshed my head with oil; my cup overflows." — (Psalms 23:5 AMP)*

The first door opened so quietly that I almost missed it.

There was no announcement, no sense of arrival, no internal swell of certainty that told me, *This is it*. It came the way many meaningful things do—through relationship, through recognition, through someone else seeing themselves reflected in words I had spoken or written, without imagining where they would land.

I wrote because He told me to, without any idea, agenda, or even an audience. My publisher asked questions to which I didn't have fully formed answers. But God had already prepared them to receive the hum of what He was forming through me before I had a completed framework with which to articulate where it was going.

My head told me *This doesn't sound professional, yet, keep this to yourself. You need to know the whole before you can share any part of it*. But control is an illusion, one I couldn't keep as a pretense in this season. The Lord opened doors to gain a publisher's interest and platform. He designed a public relations team to believe in the energy and the mission, even while they were tasked with helping me articulate the vision.

My name began to be spoken, and so did the words *radical kindness*, in rooms I didn't even know to knock. This was disorienting. Yes, there had been preparation in all of the paths: personal experience, faith, and education that led to this moment. One could quib it is evidence of preparation meeting opportunity. But it wasn't.

I noticed it only because it felt different from the doors I had knocked on before.

In earlier seasons of my life, opportunity carried urgency. When something appeared, it activated a familiar internal sequence: assess quickly, prove readiness, move fast before the moment passed. Opportunity felt like something you either seized or lost. There was pressure in that logic, and fear behind it—the fear that if you didn't move, you would be left behind. Or, if I chose to stay, it was a fear of failure if I did move.

Listening had already dismantled that posture. I didn't know what this new one was. It wasn't standing in defense. It wasn't just sitting in stillness. It was a new posture in the witness that invited a peacefully aligned movement towards something bigger than myself.

By the time doors began to open, I was no longer scanning for them. I was not positioning myself to be seen or heard. I was not rehearsing an explanation of who I was or what I had to offer. I was focusing on alignment instead of access.

That changed how I recognized what was open.

The Lord in His mercy often makes things obvious, even to me. I've spent plenty of my life in the grave and the early part of the calling, begging for a neon sign to light the way. I knew His Word is a lamp to my feet and studied it for direction. It shaped and formed me, but it was rarely the neon sign with a flashing arrow that said *This is the Way* that I wanted.

Still, other times, the Lord compels me to movement–usually at the most inconvenient times–when there is to be a promotion. The summer I spent in the inner city, attending the soul-healing retreat, asking Laura to be my mentor, freeing indentured servants, pursuing advanced degrees, and engaging in other activities. All of the times, it was a good gift I might not have seen with the eyes of my heart or an opportunity/assignment I may have missed if He hadn't insisted within my Spirit. Many other times, He's compelled me to do things my flesh would rather not, like epic forgiveness–maybe even seventy times seven times–and that too was for my good.

All of the moments were training in alignment and attunement, even when it didn't make sense. Even if my flesh found the cost too great. It was a process of me decreasing so that He could increase.

Here, in this season, I could think of a million ways I had resisted. I internally heard phrases like *delayed obedience is disobedience* as I realized I *should have* written my story long ago, like a rebellious child, with the first ask. But God doesn't shame us with condemnation. Like another trip around the mountain on the way to the Promised Land, He was merciful and gave me another opportunity, again and again.

In this season, I took one step toward obedience with my book (which was really the culmination of quite a few steps in alignment and attunement throughout my life), and He, like the Prodigal Son's father, ran to meet me and embrace me. There was no *It's about time* from Him. There was connection that never faltered, because this time, I remained. Abiding.

I was still disoriented. I would wake up and read my emails about new offers and invitations. I couldn't follow the plans for my day because divine interruptions had become part of my daily schedule now. Trauma said *The other shoe is about to fall.* Integration said *Life will go on, and things may happen, good and bad, but you belong to God, so whom shall you fear?*

The invitations that came did not feel like validation. They felt like response. Someone had read something and recognized themselves in it. Someone had heard about our mission and felt less alone. Someone wanted to keep the conversation going—not because they needed answers, but because something had shifted inside them.

I didn't pursue; I followed God's response. I learned quickly that response carries a different energy than pursuit.

Response does not rush.
Response does not require performance, which is not the same as work—I worked with fervor.
Response does not demand that you become more than you already are; it says apply who you are wholeheartedly.

I was always enough. Not too much or not enough as I'd been taught. Response simply asks whether you are willing to show up and walk in the path He provides.

Speaking engagements followed that same pattern. I did not wake up one day and decide to speak publicly about transformation. I did not create a strategy or build a platform. I responded to invitations that felt aligned with the posture I had learned to inhabit—spaces where the goal was not persuasion, but presence.

When I spoke, I noticed something else that was new. I was not trying to convince anyone.

I was not selling an idea or offering a solution. I was naming patterns I had observed and letting people locate themselves within them. The most meaningful moments were not when people nodded in agreement, but when they exhaled—sometimes visibly—as if something they had been holding could finally be set down.

That response told me more than applause ever could.

In earlier seasons, speaking required a surge of adrenaline. It demanded preparation rooted in proving competence and anticipating objections. Now, it required something else entirely: regulation. Attunement. The willingness to stay grounded in my own body while standing in front of others.

This was not easier, per se. It was truer.

I began to see how often public spaces replicate the same dynamics that stall transformation in private ones. Urgency, intensity, and performance are rewarded. Silence, slowness, and uncertainty are quietly discouraged. When those dynamics dominate, people leave with information but little capacity to integrate it.

I did not want to contribute to that.

So I spoke the way I had learned to witness: without rushing, without demanding movement, without offering answers that required people to bypass their own process. I trusted that safety would do what pressure never could. I offered an invitation. It was theirs to receive as process and progress or a seed sown that could be tended.

The response surprised me.

Not because it was large, but because it was consistent. Conversations continued long after events ended. People reached out later—not for advice, but to share what had shifted internally. Collaborations emerged organically, often with people who carried a similar posture rather than a similar résumé.

That mattered.

Collaboration felt different now, too. It is an elevated way of creating impact rather than transactions.

In the past, working with others often meant dividing labor or expanding reach. It was functional, but rarely spacious. Now, collaboration felt more like resonance—shared values, shared pace, and a shared commitment to doing work that didn't require anyone to disappear. In rooms where competition had become comfortable, taking up too much space, collaboration was now offering an alternative. A collective where individuals were celebrated, not relegated or lost.

I noticed how quickly I could discern whether a collaboration would be life-giving or depleting. It isn't just *is there reciprocity*, but also *are we going in the same direction*?

If urgency drove it, I declined.
If outcomes were prioritized without regard for process, I paused.
If the work required me to overfunction or self-erase, I said no.

That was new. Saying no did not feel like fear. It felt like stewardship.

Stewardship of my own nervous system.
Stewardship of the work itself.
Stewardship of the people who would be affected by it.

Not every door that opened was meant to be walked through. This was perhaps the most important shift of all. Without alignment and attunement, it would be hard to see the difference.

Earlier in my life, opportunity felt rare and fragile, something I had to create alone. Declining something felt risky, as if doors might not open again. That belief kept me busy, but braced, engaged, yet exhausted, far from fulfilled. Now, I trusted something different.

Alignment would continue to make space.

New chapters began to emerge in this same way—without fanfare, without force. Some were vocational, some relational, some internal. Each required discernment rather than enthusiasm. Each asked the same question in a quieter voice: *Does this deepen integration, or does it fragment it?* That question became my gatekeeper.

Walking through open doors did not mean leaving everything else behind. It meant integrating what I was learning into my daily life, work, and relationships. It meant allowing my life to expand without losing the posture that had made expansion possible.

There were moments when I felt the old reflex stir—the desire to capitalize, to scale, to move faster than wisdom allowed. Those moments were familiar, and they no longer frightened me. I had learned to notice them without obeying them. Urgency still whispered. I just didn't answer.

The work that followed—speaking, writing, collaborating, building— was no longer dependent on my endurance. It did not require me to stand watch over everything or carry outcomes on my back. Others shared the responsibility. Systems began to form that reflected the same principles I had seen at work internally: awareness, connection, movement—held together by radical kindness.

This was not a pivot away from my story. It was its continuation. One greater than I could have asked or imagined.

The doors that opened were not rewards for obedience. They were expressions of alignment. They appeared because the posture had changed, not because the effort had increased. I had not become more compelling. I had become more integrated.

That distinction matters.

Alignment does not guarantee success. It does not promise ease. I've worked long hours, but I woke up with a passion for the mission and the work I've been given to do. It does not protect against loss, because in this world, we will have tribulation.

What it offers is integrity—the ability to move through open doors without abandoning who you've been created to be along the way.

As I look back on this season, what stands out is not the opportunities themselves, but the way they arrived. Quietly. Relationally. Without requiring explanation. They asked for presence, not performance. Discernment, not urgency.

Walking through them felt less like stepping into the spotlight and more like stepping onto a path that had been there all along. A path that had been destined for me to walk long before I took my first breath. A path that had nothing to do with my own making, to God be the glory.

I did not need to know where it led.

I only needed to know how to walk.

This is how The Witness began to take shape—not as a declaration of purpose, but as a series of responses to what was already open. Doors appeared. I noticed them. Some I walked through. Some I didn't. Both choices required faith.

And for the first time, that faith no longer felt frantic or fragile. It felt grounded. It felt available. It felt like walking through a life that was no longer being pushed but gently drawn forward.

The doors I didn't open taught me as much as the ones I did.

They taught me that discernment is not about scarcity, but trust and ubiquity. That opportunity does not disappear when you slow down. That alignment creates space in ways that effort never could.

The path ahead was not fully visible. But it no longer needed to be.

"Since this is the kind of life we have chosen, the life of the Spirit, let us make sure that we do not just hold it as an idea in our heads or a sentiment in our hearts, but work out its implications in every detail of our lives. That means we will not compare ourselves with each other as if one of us were better and another worse. We have far more interesting things to do with our lives. Each of us is an original." — (Galatians 5:25-26 MSG)

CHAPTER 21

When Witness Became Shared

"Now may the God who gives endurance and who supplies encouragement grant that you be of the same mind with one another according to Christ Jesus, so that with one accord you may with one voice glorify and praise and honor the God and Father of our Lord Jesus Christ." — (Romans 15:5-6 AMP)

At first, the work was personal.

It had to be. Formation always is. What I learned to notice in myself—how safety changes perception, how kindness alters capacity, how restraint makes room for movement—could not be delegated or scaled. It had to be embodied before it could be shared.

But witness has a way of widening rather than scaling upward; especially mission-forward strategies often focus on scaling wider first.

Not demanding visibility, but because what heals one person often creates space for others to step into their own healing. Presence has a gravitational pull. When it is grounded and regulated, it invites proximity without demanding it. The natural effect is an ever-widening circle.

That invitation to wider witness changed the shape of the work. It reminded me of the Disciples being sent out two by two to spread the word, or modeling after Jesus, who disseminated a message widely without needing to scale vertically.

It began subtly. Conversations extended beyond their original boundaries. People lingered after events, not to ask questions, but to tell the truth. Small groups formed organically—not around content, but around safety and trust. I noticed that when I stayed in the posture I had learned—listening first, resisting the urge to act, and allowing the process to unfold while being peacefully aligned in movement towards something bigger than myself—others did the same.

Something collective was happening, but also something collaborative. I had not planned for that.

In earlier seasons, any expansion would have triggered control. I would have felt responsible for organizing, defining, and managing what was emerging. That instinct had served me well before; it had also exhausted me. This time, I noticed the instinct arise—and chose not to obey it.

Instead, I paid attention.

What I saw was not a demand for leadership, but a need for a framework that could become familiar and reproducible. A place where the posture we were practicing could be held consistently, without depending on any one person's endurance or availability. A structure that could protect the conditions that made transformation possible—safety, presence, restraint—without turning them into rules.

This was the moment when witness could no longer remain individual. Not because of any personal reason, but because the work itself required more than one person to hold it. I didn't know I would speak it into existence–literally–in rooms of power or on stages of influence, but I also knew it was a concept much bigger than myself. I had only been entrusted with germinating the idea.

The idea that would become The Sage Hill Project did not arrive as a vision or ambition. It emerged as recognition. I had no idea, lying flat on my broken back and trying to limp on torn hamstrings, that a book was being birthed, much less a framework or a business. I wasn't working towards anything beyond healing and obedience. Yet the conversations that gave rise to extended emails, which in turn led to invitations, refused to be ignored. A quiet acknowledgment that what had been happening informally needed a place to land. Not to be amplified, but to be named and recognized. The fledgling concept also needed to be protected.

Protection is a form of care that we rarely discuss.

We discuss building, launching, and growing. We discuss reach, impact, and sustainability. We rarely talk about what must be safeguarded so that work remains faithful to its source. I had seen too many good movements fracture under the weight of urgency and expansion. I was not interested in repeating that pattern.

What needed to be protected here was not an idea. It was a tension held between stewarding important work diligently and well, while not rushing to capitalize on a traditional vertical scale.

It was the embodiment of radical kindness that refused to coerce change. The posture of discernment that honored pace. The posture of shared responsibility that resisted hero narratives. If that posture could not be held collectively, then no structure would be worth building.

This is where "we" began to matter. Not as a rhetorical device, but as reality.

The people who gathered around this work were not looking for direction. They were looking for resonance. They recognized the same patterns I had noticed—often in their own language, through their own experiences. They had lived the cost of urgency and the relief of safety. They knew what it meant to be competent, but they were braced, capable yet depleted.

They did not need to be convinced. They needed to be supported. They needed to be equipped and empowered.

It's interesting that the first person supported was *me*. Another surprise along the way. But that support was actually a lever in widening the circle. People who not only affirmed the message and mission but were also empowered to come alongside and build. Not competitively, not with scrutiny, but with their own tools lent to the process, each according to their own time, talent, and treasure.

Some of the support came from afar, offering advice, strategy, and resources. Some became friends for the journey, a gift that counts double when you're building impact. Some friends became so collaborative that they became hype women who may have talked more about the mission of mobilizing radical kindness than I did.

Shared witness changed the way responsibility functioned. No one person carried the weight. Although I possess a gift for leadership and strategy, which enables me to make quick decisions, this organization is methodically designed as a living, breathing organism that thrives in the right environment. Decisions were made slowly. Discernment was more communal. Boundaries were not negotiable or performative; they were assumed. The work expanded because capacity expanded—not because pressure demanded it.

This was unfamiliar territory.

I had been part of teams and organizations before. Many of them were effective. Few of them were regulated. Fear lived just beneath the surface, shaping decisions in ways no one dared to name out loud. Urgency was often mistaken for leadership. Exhaustion was praised as commitment.

I did not want to recreate that. I kept saying that witness had me standing at the intersection of my lived experiences, faith, and education. Now, I knew better, so I had to do better. Legacies are born through intentionality and hard work. That doesn't mean we have to do it all at once, and it doesn't mean we have to do more or essentially *strike while the iron is hot* because we weren't selling anything. We were inspiring and facilitating a movement.

So we did less.

We slowed meetings. We resisted timelines that did not respect process. We named when energy shifted and paused accordingly. We chose clarity over speed and consent over compliance. These choices were not always efficient.

They were faithful.

What surprised me most was the amount of creativity that emerged once the pressure was removed. When people no longer felt evaluated or rushed, they offered more—not less. They brought ideas without needing approval. They shared concerns before they hardened into conflict. They trusted the group to hold complexity without requiring immediate resolution.

Safety had done its work again.

The Sage Hill Project became a place where witness was not something one person embodied on behalf of others, but something practiced together. A place where radical kindness was not an initiative, but a practice. Where people were not asked to perform transformation, but were given space to engage with it honestly.

This was not a pivot away from personal witness. It was its natural extension.

Earlier in my life, collective work had often cost me something I did not yet know how to protect. I would absorb what others could not hold. I would overfunction to maintain stability. I would mistake indispensability for impact.

This time, shared witness meant shared limits.

Similar to Sage Hill Consulting, which focuses on consulting and coaching as agents of change, we recognized that this something could not depend on one person. We noticed that when dynamics replicated old patterns and addressed them early. We refused to spiritualize exhaustion or excuse behavior that undermined safety. We held one another accountable to the posture that had made the work possible in the first place.

Accountability, I learned, feels very different in a regulated system.

It is not threatening.
It is not shaming.
It is not corrective in the punitive sense.

It is orienting. Accountability is enabled by agreed-upon expectations.

This was the strategy presented to clients seeking change in organizational design at Sage Hill Consulting. The application at The Sage Hill Project provided a point of emphasis for putting into practice excerpts from a larger, Integrative Transformation Blueprint™.

The framework was designed to facilitate lasting change in individuals, even the most fragmented, with wider implications that could be experimented with in real-time through a formal and informal network of collaboration.

When someone drifted toward urgency, the group slowed. When someone carried more than their share, the group redistributed the load. When fear surfaced, it was named—not judged—and given time to settle before decisions were made. This did not discount the need for reciprocity, but rather highlighted the premise that everyone must contribute, or the group's sense of safety would be at risk.

This way of working required trust.

Trust that alignment would outlast pressure.

Trust that clarity would emerge without force.

Trust that people would rise to responsibility when they were not coerced into it, but rather invited to operate where it was safe to be curious. It was safe to fail forward. And when connections were the norm and not the exception.

That trust was not naïve. It was informed by everything I had seen about how transformation actually happens. Shared witness also changed how I understood leadership.

Leadership here did not appear to be direction. It seemed to be holding space to facilitate inquiry and creativity. It did not require answers so much as attunement. The most influential moments were often the quietest—when someone noticed a shift in the room, named it gently, and allowed the group to respond.

This kind of leadership does not draw attention to itself. It creates conditions in which others can lead themselves and others, informally and formally. It frees the leader to scan the horizon and adjust the sails while others operate congruently within the predefined culture.

As the fledgling collaborations continued, I became aware of a deeper shift taking place within me. I no longer felt responsible for outcomes as much as for conditions. That distinction relieved a pressure I had carried for most of my life.

Outcomes belong to God, time, context, and choice. Conditions belong to stewardship. When witness became shared, stewardship became collective.

I did not need to be everywhere to promote the project, because seeds were planted in one room and carried by others to be sown elsewhere. I did not personally need to speak into every moment because others were carrying the message out of the room with them. I did not need to protect the work by controlling it. In fact, control would have undermined the very thing we were trying to preserve.

Letting go was not a loss. It was alignment. And that attunement and alignment with God's vision placed in my heart was freeing.

There were moments when I felt the old reflex return—the desire to define, to clarify, to ensure the work was understood correctly. Each time, I returned to the same question that had guided me since The Calling:

Does this deepen integration, or does it fragment it?

That question doesn't fail.

Shared witness requires ongoing discernment in collaboration. It is not static. It evolves as people grow, as contexts change, as new challenges emerge, and as individuals who do not yet share the mission attempt to alter their dynamics with a different approach. What they don't know is that what remains constant is the posture—the commitment to safety, presence, and radical kindness as non-negotiables.

You cannot take one vehicle in two different directions; therefore, some people may travel parallel for a while, and we wish them well, but they may not be on the same journey as us or at the same time. And that too is a shift to bless those who are on their own journey and cheer them on their way without losing anything from our own. That too is part of letting go and maintaining a peaceful posture in movement.

This is not the end of the work.

The work has always been bigger than me. I *get* to do this. And now, *we* get to do this together. Collaboratively. We are agents of change and legacy changers because there is a language and a framework, a blueprint to follow.

This is clarification. I am part of the witness, not its container. My responsibility is to stay aligned, to remain attentive, and to release control when it threatens attunement.

Witness became shared not because I was finished, but because the work had outgrown individual ownership.

That is how I knew it was real.

If what had emerged could be held by many without losing its integrity, then it had moved beyond testimony. It had become practice. It had become something that could live in rooms I would never enter, in conversations I would never hear, in lives that would never know my name.

That was not frightening. It was freeing. Shared witness does not require me to be present everywhere. It requires me to trust what presence has already made possible.

And that trust has changed everything.

"It was for this freedom that Christ set us free [completely liberating us]; therefore keep standing firm and do not be subject again to a yoke of slavery [which you once removed]."
— (Galatians 5:1 AMP)

CHAPTER 22

Living Raised

"Since then, you have been raised with Christ—set your hearts on things above, where Christ is, seated at the right hand of God." — (Colossians 3:1)

Being raised did not deliver me into clarity. It delivered me into responsibility.

Not the kind of responsibility that announces itself or demands immediate action, but the quieter kind—the kind that asks whether I will live from what I now know, especially in relationship, especially when misunderstanding is possible, especially when there is no visible outcome attached. The kind that requires fidelity rather than force.

With the Sage Hill Project and its mission to mobilize radical kindness becoming reality, I often found myself saying *I'm not the kindest person I know.* It seemed like a disclaimer, as the representative promoting radical kindness, that my own flawed and traumatized existence had allowed the pattern to emerge, and that it was through the efforts of others toward me, who were much kinder than I, that my transformation was enabled.

For a long time, I believed resurrection would feel decisive. Dropping the grave clothes and being called forth should arrive with some sort of pomp and circumstance. I imagined it as an arrival point, a moment after which things would finally make sense, or at least settle and become easier. Instead, being raised has felt more like learning to live without the scaffolding that once held me upright. The supports I relied on—hypervigilance, overfunctioning, endurance—were never meant to be permanent structures. They kept me alive–in survival mode. They did not teach me how to really *live* with myself and others, to thrive.

Living raised has meant discovering that healing is not sustained by intensity. It is sustained by alignment—especially relational alignment and attunement that begin with vertical connection to God.

In earlier seasons, my faith had been measured by output. By how much I could hold, what I could endure, how many people I could support, and how efficiently I could respond when something broke. Responsibility had been my reflex out of obligation and necessity, not rooted in a relationship. It gave shape to my days and meaning to my exhaustion. It also shaped my relationships in ways I could not see at the time. I was reliable. I was present. I was capable. I was also often unavailable to receive...compliments, feedback, love, and support.

Listening and stillness began to expose that imbalance.

Not through confrontation, but through contrast. The Grave analysis helped understand how and why my brain was wired for such responses. The Calling highlighted the moments when someone stayed present without asking me to perform, conversations that did not escalate–even when I did not immediately respond, and through relationships that did not withdraw when I named a limit instead of a solution.

We named this transformation as possible through the radical kindness of others toward me, which created space for me to receive God's radical kindness, allowing me to apply it inwardly and be radically kind to myself. This increased my capacity to be radically kind to others and, like ripples in the water from the stone of radical kindness being cast, seeds of hope that enable transformation were sown.

Now, living raised requires restraint. We maintain the momentum gained through radical kindness and add restraint to it. This directly correlates to ceasing judgment towards ourselves and others, which is not the same as being convicted and developing ourselves. It is:

Restraint from fixing what is not mine to fix.

Restraint from filling the silence to avoid discomfort.

Restraint from offering wisdom before safety has been established.

Restraint from rumination of the things I and others have done or left undone.

Restraint from the condemnation that practice can bring.

Restraint from catastrophizing the future based on the lies trauma tells.

This restraint has been most tested throughout the three forms of connection: vertical, inward, and outward.

Restraint is the expansion of intention. There is no need for restraint if there is no power to cause damage. Restraint is the disciplined capacity to pause, discern, and act in alignment with one's values, wisdom, and long-term purpose, rather than succumbing to immediate urges or external pressure. The counterfeit of this practice in the unhealed version of ourselves may manifest as passivity, avoidance, repression of emotions, people-pleasing, or fear-based silence.

Restraint in vertical connection is actually choosing surrender when we would prefer control. It is choosing to show up and be present in our inner gardens, where we commune with an ever-present God, the embodiment of love and radical kindness, when it is easier to give in to busyness and distractions that affirm "my will be done" rather than "Thy will be done." Restraint here models the wisdom of Proverbs 3:5, which Laura used as a mantra in teaching it to me: "Lean not on your own understanding." Restraint in vertical connection lays the foundation of trust – a faith in what the eyes of our head cannot see, as we follow using our spiritual eyes instead.

For me, inward restraint made a bold move towards silencing the relentless inner critic that pushed me toward perfectionism, while extending grace to everyone else. Restraint expands the intention of choosing fledgling neuropathways of health and function rather than the well-worn, dysfunctional, or disordered pathways forged by trauma. Restraint meant seeing through my own faults to my own needs and extending grace, which can still be held in balance with accountability and growth.

That peace that begins with radical kindness and restraint, initiated vertically and applied inwardly, influences how we attend to others in our outward connections. There is significant overlap among all three connections as we cease to compare our best with their worst, vice versa, or silence the voice of comparison completely–an extension of judgment. When we cease judging others' actions, we make space to love without condition. Their dysregulated choices and actions no longer need to affect us personally. Our boundaries maintain our state of safety while still allowing love to flow outward toward them.

Inherent in restraint is the spirit of curiosity that engages before reaction has a chance to be expressed.

There were moments when someone I cared about was struggling, and every instinct in me wanted to intervene—to organize, to problem-solve, to carry what felt too heavy for them to hold alone. In earlier seasons, that instinct would have been praised. It would have been interpreted as a sign of compassion, leadership, or faithfulness. Living raised asked a different question: *Is my help being requested—or is my nervous system responding to discomfort?* This can be the threshold where helping is no longer helpful, though the world may fail to see the subtle distinction, our nervous system and our body keep the score.

Sometimes, the most faithful response was simply being present without direction. Sometimes it was listening without resolution–inviting stillness, whether they chose to inhibit it or not. Sometimes it was staying close while allowing another person to find their own footing.

That kind of restraint felt risky.

It required trusting that relationship does not collapse without control. It required believing that love can exist without management. It required letting go of the belief that being needed was the same as being connected. And it gave up the need to control outcomes, letting life unfold on its own pathway and timeline, which is not the same as living aimlessly.

Living raised has meant learning how to stay in relationship without overfunctioning, for myself or others.

It seems only accurate to reiterate that I am not the kindest person I know. Lest I paint the picture of an arrival destination rather than a journey. Irrational irritations, such as zipper merges, left-lane impediments, abandoned grocery carts, and my own reaction to others' judgment, among others, provide opportunities for me to act on a new neuropathway or on the well-worn path of reaction. The journey and evolution of self this side of Heaven is continual, for all of us.

However, it is also important to celebrate the small shifts that become new practices, translated into a lifestyle that aligns with our values. Raise the Ebenezer. Mark the milestones. We're only human, after all, and transformation requires consistent, hard work over time.

However, the shifts changed how I showed up in conversations as I began to notice how often I anticipated needs before they were expressed, how quickly I filled pauses, and how reflexively I took responsibility for outcomes that were never mine to carry. These habits were not born out of arrogance. They were born out of survival. They had once protected connection by preventing conflict or disappointment. Sometimes it was a lack of capacity to teach someone or walk beside someone who had yet to learn a different way, and so I attempted to do it for them.

It took courage to keep going–surviving–while in the Grave. It took courage to make a decision and take one step out of the grave as I was called forth. Another type of courage to embrace my Calling. And still a new courage was needed in the Witness as I lived raised.

But living raised has required a different kind of courage—the courage to let relationships breathe. To open my hands of what I was holding onto so I could receive what the Lord had, not only for me, but also to let life unfold for others.

There were moments when someone misinterpreted my restraint as distance. Moments when slowing down disrupted patterns others had come to rely on. Moments when I wasn't rushing to fix things felt like abandonment—to them or to me. These moments revealed how deeply urgency had shaped not only my own behavior but the relational ecosystems I had been part of.

Living raised did not ask me to correct those misunderstandings immediately. It asked me to stay regulated enough to withstand them.

That has been one of the most relationally transformative aspects of this season: learning that I can remain present even when I am misunderstood, and that relationship can survive tension without immediate resolution.

What surprised me most was how much capacity returned once I stopped living in reaction. When my nervous system was no longer braced for constant relational impact, I had more space to be curious rather than defensive. I could listen without rehearsing a response. I could tolerate pauses without assuming something was wrong. I could engage in disagreement without needing to resolve it in real time.

That kind of presence changed the quality of my relationships.

Yes, attacks of others still can be triggering for my well-trained trauma responses and CPTSD, or rejection sensitivity through ADHD. But I have tools, a framework, and a system that allow self-regulation to prevail more quickly than ever before. This system was laid decades ago, and during my formative years. Emerging from the grave did not erase that process or programming, but it did transform what is possible and provide alternative pathways, equipping and empowering me with more choice in my responses.

Conversations slowed. Depth replaced urgency. Trust grew—not because I was doing more, but because I was doing less *intentionally*. People began sharing more freely, not because I had answers, but because I was no longer rushing them toward conclusions.

Living raised has reshaped how I understand faithfulness in community.

Faithfulness, I have learned, is not measured by how much we carry for others. It is measured by how well we discern what we are meant to hold together—and what each person must carry for themselves. It asks whether we can remain connected without becoming fused, supportive without becoming indispensable. Boundaries created safety as they replaced codependent triangles that had become easier to spot, and allowed me to be further empowered by refusing engagement that had once come so naturally.

These were new boundaries—not as walls, but as containers.

Boundaries that protect attention.
Boundaries that preserve mutuality.
Boundaries that allow truth to surface without coercion.

In earlier seasons, boundaries felt relationally dangerous. They felt like withdrawal, or worse, rejection. I worried that saying no would fracture the connection, that slowing down would be seen as disappointing, and that choosing rest would be misread as disengagement. Living raised taught me that boundaries do not weaken healthy relationships—they clarify them.

They reveal who can remain present when roles shift. They also helped me operate from a well-defined position. This practice actually expands healthy interactions, making health and function more available to others, not less.

This clarity was not always comfortable. Some relationships adjusted. Some resisted. Some fell away. None of this was dramatic or sudden. It unfolded quietly, through small choices repeated over time. By saying, *I can't do that right now,* without apology. Through choosing honesty over accommodation. Through allowing others to step forward instead of stepping in myself.

Living raised has meant trusting that connection rooted in safety does not require constant maintenance. It was understanding emotional object permanence with ADHD and working *with* my brain rather than *against* it from a place of condemnation and judgment. There was a balance to develop communication around capacity in ways that managed expectations. Some understood, and some didn't. Open hands that partner with alignment and attunement made space for that to be okay. Connection requires intentional effort, but not draining work. Taking the time to decide which people brought energy and which drained it led to conscious decisions about with whom I spent my time and when.

There is a particular vulnerability that comes with living raised in community: the temptation to translate integration into instruction. To assume that because something has become clear to us, it must be made clear to others. I have felt that pull—to explain my boundaries, to justify my pace, to offer frameworks where presence might be enough.

But witness, at its most faithful, resists that impulse. It operates in a place of acceptance, of myself and others, where their input does not impact my state of being.

Witness does not rush formation.
It does not demand agreement.
It allows people to encounter truth at the pace safety allows.

Living raised has meant trusting that what has been integrated will reveal itself relationally, without explanation. If the above state of being felt like walking away or abandonment, let me challenge that notion as a place of control. To the contrary, integrated transformation allows us to sit in stillness protected by healthy boundaries, whether others choose the same state or not.

Sound psychological practice requires acknowledging that sometimes we are simply there to sow the seed, and the relationship lasts but a moment. It also gives the disclaimer that abusive relationships may require separation. But the kind of radical kindness, restraint, and patience we're talking about is applied to most relationships and people we encounter in our lives.

This is where trust has been tested in ordinary moments. In conversations that ended without closure. In relationships that require patience rather than progress. In seasons where faithfulness looked less like momentum and more like maintenance—showing up consistently, listening carefully, and staying grounded even when nothing appeared to be changing.

Those moments revealed something essential: resurrection is not sustained by novelty. It is sustained by repetition. By choosing, again and again, to respond rather than react. To stay present rather than perform. To allow relationship to mature without forcing outcomes.

Some days, living raised feels almost indistinguishable from living at all. There are meals to share, misunderstandings to navigate, disappointments to hold. There is nothing extraordinary about these moments. And yet, they are the proving ground.

Because living raised is not about extraordinary faith. It is about ordinary faithfulness practiced in relationship.

It is about noticing when old relational patterns resurface and choosing not to automatically obey them, and keeping a short account when they do. It is about recognizing when the body tightens in conversation and staying present anyway. It is about allowing others to be who they are, even when that means tolerating difference, ambiguity, or unresolved tension.

This kind of living requires humility.

Humility to admit when I am tired.
Humility to say when I don't know.
Humility to trust that relationship does not depend on my performance.

It also requires courage—the courage to remain visible without managing perception, to remain engaged without controlling outcomes, to remain faithful without ensuring results.

Living raised has not simplified my relationships. It has deepened them.

As the representative for the movement to mobilize radical kindness. I needed to articulate the process, the findings, and the framework. The Sage Hill Project is evolving at its own pace. A growth chart can't predict when it will hit milestones and at what magnitude. However, the project is grounded in the revealed truth that creates space for discussion and further refinement as others provide their own testimonies to The Witness.

That is what resurrection has looked like for me.

Not escape from the grave, but freedom from its relational authority.
Not immunity from rupture, but the capacity to repair.
Not a platform, but a posture that creates space for others to stand—or sit in stillness—or be aligned with their peace in movement—wherever they are in their journey, there is space to belong.

Living raised is not the end of the story. It is the way the story continues—between people, over time, and in the quiet faithfulness of relationship.

And it is from here that witness begins to move outward again—not as urgency, not as obligation, but as invitation.

"When He had finished speaking, He said to Simon [Peter], 'Put out into the deep water and lower your nets for a catch [of fish]." Simon replied, 'Master, we worked hard all night [to the point of exhaustion] and caught nothing [in our nets], but at Your word I will [do as you say and] lower the nets [again].' When they had done this, they caught a great number of fish, and their nets [at the point of] breaking; so they signaled to their partners in the other boat to come and help them. And they came and filled both of the boats [with fish], so that they began to sink."
— (Luke 5:5-7 AMP)

CHAPTER 23

A Life That Moves

"Do you show contempt for the riches of His kindness, forbearance, and patience, not realizing that God's kindness is intended to lead you to repentance?"
— (Romans 2:4)

For much of my life, movement meant escape.

It meant leaving danger, outrunning pain, staying one step ahead of what might collapse if I slowed down. Movement was a reflex before it became a choice. It was how I survived.

Even in faith, movement carried urgency. I believed obedience should feel decisive. That transformation would arrive with clarity or conviction sharp enough to compel change. I assumed repentance required confrontation—something firm enough to interrupt the momentum of old patterns.

It's not that living raised as a witness removes movement from my life. It transforms it.

What I have come to understand—slowly, and with great mercy—is that transformation does not occur through force. It unfolds through conditions. Through the environment Paul describes in Romans 2:4, patience, restraint, and kindness, truth becomes safe and can emerge. This insight both reframed and brought together everything I thought I knew about change.

Repentance is not a moment.

It is not a collapse.

It is not a demand.

It is an invitation to movement that becomes possible when safety is sustained long enough for truth to take root. Repentance, mentioned by Paul and elsewhere, is literally a change of direction. It is turning from following our own ways and turning back to God. This movement is facilitated by kindness, restraint, and patience.

There is a profound, inseparable correlation between repentance and transformation. Repentance is the doorway through which lies the house of transformation. Said differently, repentance is the gate through which we enter the inner garden and find transformation. We can be transformed by the renewing of our minds (Romans 12:2). The Greek word for repentance is *metanoia*, which literally translates to a change of mind, leading to a changed heart, which in turn leads to a changed direction, resulting in transformed living. It's an awareness or remembering of who we are in God.

Transformation begins with a new identity, not behavior. It is the realization of who we are created to be, regardless of what we've done or left undone. This isn't self-help; it is being made new. This is why transformation can't be earned or forced—it is *received*. For this reason, the people who come with kindness, restraint, and patience are gifts along the way that people can choose to receive on their transformational journey.

In this environment, transformation isn't just a grand, nebulous idea, but a valid invitation that may be received and acted upon. The Greek word for transformation used by Paul in Romans 12:2 is *metamorphoō,* a deep structural change. Our brains, which were created for connection, rewired for protection through trauma, or disrupted through disordered thinking, actually experience structural change through this framework of transformation.

This sustainable change requires two parts: relationship and participation. A relationship with transformed individuals can foster an environment where awareness of the need for change is cultivated, and the belief in the possibility of change is instilled. Then relationships occurring across the connections: vertical, inward, and outward, further the process of change and the sustainability of transformation. Transformation is not solitary, but it is participatory. A willingness to surrender, to sit with discomfort, and make posture adjustments as one moves into alignment and attunement with God becomes the hallmark of the intention put into motion.

Transformation is progressive, not instant. Perhaps this is why one of the process's descriptors is patience. For those of us who struggle with immediate resolutions, this may be how we've gotten derailed by past endeavors.

In high school, I received kindness, restraint, and patience from people like Sally Shipley, but lacked the framework to sustain it. I quit the process because, though I was partially aware, I didn't understand it and thought willpower alone would suffice. Laura's divine interruption was the consistent space held over time that allowed a new practice to take shape. The framework was largely developed here, unbeknownst to me at the time, and I experienced a significant transformation. But there were many ebbs and flows to my progress, which is often not linear, because of my own wandering heart that had to repent (change directions) again and again through lack of patience in the process.

The frustration in my own progress was compounded by my all-or-nothing attitude. I am all-in or all-out for most things in life. My own growth and maturity are evidenced by my understanding that rarely are extremes healthy and functional, but rather a moderate middle ground is where balance is found (this isn't true in all instances; all life-sweeping generalities will yield error in specifics-nevertheless, I'm saying: generally speaking, this is applicable). From this place also grows the ability to engage others with a spirit of curiosity rather than coercion that battles for "who's right."

This is where *The Witness* has been leading all along.

The grave trained us to move quickly. To react. To protect. To act before something worse could happen. In the grave, patience is dangerous. Stillness feels like exposure. Restraint looks like neglect.

But resurrection does not call us back into urgency. It teaches us how to move patiently in a world addicted to speed.

What became clear over time was that patience did not remove responsibility. It redefined it.

When urgency no longer governs our movement, we become responsible for something far less visible and far more demanding: **the conditions we create for others**. The emotional climate we bring into rooms. The pace we establish in conversation. The way we handle tension without escalating it. The way we allow discomfort to exist without rushing to manage it away. This does not mean we are responsible for others' reactions or their emotions.

This is the responsibility of a raised life—not to produce change (the only one we can change is ourselves), but to become a place where change is possible.

I am responsible now for how I move among people. For whether my presence increases pressure or relieves it. For whether my responses invite honesty or shut it down. For whether patience governs my pace, even when speed would be rewarded...if only internally.

This responsibility does not announce itself. It arrives quietly, through repeated choices that few notice and no one applauds. But once it becomes clear, it cannot be unseen.

The calling brought awareness. It taught me to notice what was happening beneath the surface—how my body responded, how my faith functioned, how old agreements still shaped my interpretations. Awareness did not require action. It required honesty and the ability not to flinch at what I saw. It required acknowledging what had transpired and what had not, without whitewashing what was and without minimizing the good or the bad. It was a neutral assessment of the past and the present that yielded the barest hope in what could be.

Connection followed. Not connection as agreement or closeness, but as sustained presence. The kind of presence that does not rush discomfort away. The kind that allows truth to be spoken without consequence. An abiding presence with God, my Redeemer and my Sustainer, developed. I learned more about who I was created to be and how, not only I, but others process and interpret information differently. How diversity, by design and collaboration, is a reflection of the kind of safety that makes the most creative and productive teams.

And then, without announcement, movement changed.

Not into effort.
Not into striving.
But into alignment.

Movement, I learned, is not what we do next. It is how we live once truth and safety have learned to coexist.

This is the movement of a raised life. Alignment with peace as a practice, which is not passive, and attunement with its Author. It is visible not in urgency, but in patience. Not in correction, but in restraint. Not in persuasion, but in kindness that does not need to explain itself.

This kind of movement is disruptive in its own way. Disorienting to those who are used to being on the outside looking in, and to those who wear impenetrable armor as a badge. The motive of movement distinguishes it from other engagements in social justice or ministry. Rather than "fixing" a problem or needing to be responsible for outcomes, it comes alongside those suffering with the stillness we've embodied that invites something to shift.

It unsettles systems built on pressure. It challenges leadership that equates speed with faithfulness. It exposes how often urgency masquerades as obedience.

A life that moves patiently cannot be rushed, though it consistently and dependably stewards the work given with higher efficiency than the norm.
A presence shaped by kindness cannot be weaponized, and they cease to receive the arrows thrown at them as personal attacks.
A witness grounded in restraint cannot be co-opted by fear, because their surrender of control is, perhaps, the highest measure of self-control.

This is why witness matters. Witness is not proclamation. It is not instruction. It is not visibility.

Witness is what repentance looks like once it has been embodied through the process of transformation.

When a life moves differently—when it does not react where it once would have, when it does not escalate where it once needed control, when it does not withdraw where it once feared exposure—transformation is already underway.

This is not theoretical.

I have seen it in rooms where no one was trying to change. In conversations that slowed instead of hardened. In leadership spaces where patience altered the atmosphere and produced a changed culture more than authority ever did, often by informal leaders whose influence is not relegated to a role.

When kindness is sustained, people tell the truth, beginning with themselves–vulnerability.
When restraint is practiced, trust emerges, allowing us to drop our masks and attempt authenticity.
When patience is embodied, movement follows with permission to fail forward *together*.

Not forced movement. Chosen movement. Intentional steps in a strategic direction to claim a life of abundance this side of Heaven.

The world teaches us that change must be immediate to be real. That delay equals disobedience. That clarity must precede action.

But resurrection teaches something else.

It teaches us that God is not in a hurry. That transformation unfolds at the pace safety allows. That kindness does work pressure cannot. This is not passive faith. It is disciplined faith. That makes space for ourselves and others to heed the original call of Jesus *to come*. Just as we are–just as *they* are and receive. To lay down what we are holding onto so that we can receive what the Lord has for us. Then, we extend the invitation to others, with no timeline or agenda. The invitation comes not with words, but by a presence marked by kindness, patience, and restraint. The Great Commission is actually a movement towards those who would push love away more than it ever has been mere words in a sermon.

It takes discipline to remain patient when the world's economy rewards urgency. To stay restrained when reaction would feel justified. To trust kindness when control would feel safer.

This is the work of witness.

Not telling people how to move—but showing them it is possible to move differently and extending grace so they can realize it in their time.

I no longer believe repentance begins with correction, not in some theological heretical way. But, through the actual model provided by Jesus to those who were far from God. Seeing through the fault to the need. Sitting with them in their misery and crossing all social norms and boundaries to make them feel seen, heard, and valued in a way that creates a sense of belonging–connection.

I believe it begins when someone encounters a life that no longer operates from fear. Fear of judgment. Fear of condemnation. Fear of being ostracized. Fear of being seen as less than. What could you do with your raised life if fear were no longer an issue? What could we do together?

A life that does not need to prove itself. A presence that does not escalate tension. A movement that does not demand results.

That kind of witness does not announce itself. There's no need to. It lingers. It creates space. It invites others to notice what they have been carrying—and gently asks whether they still need to. If there is a commission here, it is not a task. It is an invitation to live patiently enough that others can change without being pushed. To practice restraint in a culture addicted to reaction. To embody kindness where judgment would be easier. To trust that movement shaped by alignment will outlast movement driven by force.

Witness is not the end of transformation. It is not a destination in which we arrive, but rather a state we find ourselves living in as a result of transformation. It is transformation learned well enough to be lived publicly—without performance, without urgency, without fear.

This is the life of the raised. Not because it is perfect. Perfect is an illusion for all but One. But because it moves differently.

And that difference—radical kindness, restraint, and patience—is how resurrection continues in the world.

"My dear children, let's not just talk about love; let's practice real love. This is the only way we'll know we're living truly, living in God's reality. It's also the way to shut down debilitating self-criticism, even when there is something to it. For God is greater than our worried hearts and knows more about us than we do ourselves. And friends, once that's taken care of and we're no longer accusing or condemning ourselves, we're bold and free before God! We're able to stretch our hands out and receive what we asked for because we're doing what He said, doing what pleases Him." — (1 John 3:18-22 MSG)

Conclusion

There is a moment in every resurrection story when movement changes.

Not because the miracle ends, but because it has already happened.

The stone has been rolled away. Breath has returned. Life has re-entered what was once sealed. And still—there is a pause. A moment where recognition settles in before anything is asked.

This is that moment.

You have stood in the grave and then walked out.
You have learned to sit in the calling.
You have learned how a raised life moves differently in the witness.

Not quickly.
Not loudly.
Not under pressure.

But kindly. With restraint. And, patiently.

If this book has done its work, it has not convinced you of anything new. It has helped you recognize what you already know in your body, mind, and spirit. It has named the cost of urgency. It has shown you that survival, while necessary, is not the same as living, and certainly different than thriving. And it has revealed that transformation does not happen through force—but through the sustained conditions that make truth bearable and transformation possible.

This is where commission begins.

In Scripture, resurrection is never the end of the story. It is the turning point where responsibility shifts—not toward performance, but toward stewardship.

Jesus does not rush those He raises. He does not immediately explain. He does not demand proof. He allows recognition to come first. Assimilation to take hold. Only then does He send.

Go.
Tell.
Feed.
Witness.

Not as pressure—but as overflow.

Psychologically, this matters.

Change that is rushed does not last. Coerced transformation does not integrate. When fear drives movement, the nervous system returns to survival—even if the language is spiritual. But when kindness creates safety, the mind becomes curious instead of defensive. The body softens instead of bracing for impact. The heart opens instead of hiding.

This is why Scripture tells us that it is God's kindness that leads to repentance.

Not shame.
Not urgency.
Not correction.

Kindness.

Once you know this, movement is no longer neutral.

How you move matters.
The pace you set matters.
The tone you carry into rooms matters.
The way you handle tension—whether you escalate it or hold it—matters.

This is not a call to do more. It is a call to live and move differently.

Wherever you are on your transformation journey, keep one hand outstretched ahead of you to be mentored and to grow. Living things continue to grow; stagnation brings death and a slippery slide back into the grave. With the other hand, keep extending grace and intention towards others. Let each hand be guided with kindness, restraint, and patience.

You are now responsible—not for outcomes, not for changing others, not for fixing what is broken—but for the conditions you create.

You are responsible for whether your presence increases pressure or relieves it.
For whether your responses invite honesty in safety or shut it down.
For whether patience governs your pace, even when speed would earn approval.

This is the work of witness.

Witness is not proclamation.
It is not persuasion.
It is not visibility.

Witness is the lived evidence that a raised life moves through the world without force.

It is kindness practiced long enough to become trustworthy.

It is restraint where reaction would be easier.
It is patience sustained when nothing appears to be changing.

This kind of witness will be misunderstood at times. It will be mistaken for disengagement. It will not always produce immediate fruit. But it will endure.

Because what changes slowly integrates deeply. The first step before operating in kindness, restraint, and patience is to divest yourself of judgment toward yourself and others (Romans 2:1-3).

You are not commissioned to convince.
You are not commissioned to correct.
You are not commissioned to hurry anyone—including yourself.

You are commissioned to create spaces through presence and interaction that enable transformation.

To steward the safety you have learned to live in. To carry patience into a hurried world. To embody kindness in spaces shaped by fear.

This is how resurrection continues.

Not through spectacle. Not through systems. But through lives that move differently once they have been raised.

If you are reading this and recognizing yourself—your patterns, your exhaustion, your longing—then the story has already begun to widen — reaching towards a transformed life. You do not need permission to move differently. You have already been changed, and you will continue to change.

And if you are wondering what comes next, the answer is simpler than you may expect.

You live.

Attentively.
Faithfully.
With awareness of your pace.

You live a raised life that is radically kind and marked by restraint and patience.

Because you are no longer who you were.

You are whom He raised.

Where the Conversation Continues

This book was never meant to be the end of a conversation.

It was meant to open one.

If you have finished these pages feeling seen, unsettled, clarified, or quietly stirred, that response matters to me. Not because it needs to be managed or directed, but because it tells me the work is alive. Transformation rarely announces itself loudly. More often, it appears as a question you can no longer ignore, or a way of moving that no longer suits you.

For many readers, this book will be enough. It will do its work privately, over time, as a confirmation and a plumb line. That is not only acceptable—it is faithful.

But some of you may sense that the conversation is still unfolding.

You may be navigating leadership, ministry, caregiving, education, or systems shaped by urgency and wondering how to live differently *within* them. You may be seeking language for what you've lived, or structure for a transformation you can feel but not yet articulate. You may be longing for spaces where patience, kindness, and restraint are not sidelined, but practiced.

If that is you, I want you to know that you are not alone—and that this work does continue.

Over time, the ideas and practices woven throughout this book have taken shape beyond these pages through **The Sage Hill Project**—a space dedicated to cultivating an integrated, embodied, and sustainable transformation. This work appears in many forms because transformation does not reside in a single context.

The conversation continues through:

- **Speaking events and sermons**: where these themes are explored in communities, conferences, and gatherings seeking depth rather than urgency, and include the Integrative Transformation Blueprint™, mobilizing radical kindness, moving from transactional to transformational leadership, slaying the bullies–beginning with ourselves, how to avoid moving from the hero to the villain in conflict resolution, and how to move others toward societal change.

- **One-on-One and Group Coaching:** co-creates space where safety and guidance foster breakthroughs in awareness, connection, and movement that facilitate desired outcomes through integration and integrity across every area of an individual's life and, corporately, through congruent narratives across team and organizational experiences.

- **Retreats**: designed to create the conditions for listening, restoration, and embodied awareness away from the pressures of performance.

- **Corporate and Ministerial Consulting:** coming alongside leaders to assess themselves, their systems, and their teams to optimize culture in ways that increase creativity, productivity, and engagement.

- **Corporate and organizational workshops**: supporting leaders and teams navigating burnout, culture change, and trauma-informed leadership with guidance and tools for immediate application and impact.

- **Campus workshops**: engaging students and educators in conversations around identity, resilience, and sustainable formation, including slaying bullies and mobilizing radical kindness. We also offer customized Kindness Labs Live for student-led organizations that emphasize internal and outward connections, align with the movement, address execution challenges, and provide ways to apply the tools provided.
- **Book clubs and small groups**: where this material is processed communally, at a pace that honors safety and honest reflection and invites a movement toward radical kindness.

In the coming seasons, this work will also expand into **curriculum and training pathways** designed to equip others who feel called to steward transformation in their own spheres of influence. These programs will offer education and certification for those seeking to become **coaches trained in the Integrative Transformation Blueprint™**—not as a technique, but as a way of cultivating awareness, connection, and movement with integrity and care.

This is meant as a global movement to mobilize radical kindness. This is not about replication.

It is about multiplication that respects context, honors limits, and prioritizes safety in ways that transform individuals, changes families, changes legacies, and ultimately shapes culture and transforms society.

If you choose to engage further, you will find invitations—not expectations. Spaces for conversation—not performance. A shared commitment to transformation that does not rely on force, urgency, or spectacle.

You can learn more, connect, or follow the ongoing work through **The Sage Hill Project (www.thesagehillproject.com),** where events and further works will be updated. There, you can also subscribe to our newsletter to keep up-to-date and engage as a thought partner.

Wherever this book meets you, my hope is the same:

That you continue to move patiently.
That you steward the kindness you have learned.
That you trust the pace of transformation—yours and others'.

Thank you for walking with me through these pages, and for believing that change is possible, starting with ourselves.

With Gratitude,

— Melissa

Scan the QR code to continue the conversation and join the global movement to mobilize radical kindness.

About the Author

Melissa Swonger is a keynote speaker, bestselling author, trauma-informed coach, and qualitative researcher dedicated to helping people reclaim their lives through transformational healing, fierce love, and bold kindness. As a Ph.D. candidate in Psychology, she draws from both lived experience and academic research to illuminate the intersection of trauma, identity, leadership, and spiritual renewal. Her work is devoted to those navigating deep pain, chronic stress, and identity fragmentation—offering hope, tools, and a way forward. This often translates into leadership development and into educating, equipping, and empowering people to create a culture, both internally and externally, that facilitates transformation.

Melissa is the founder of The Sage Hill Project, a movement mobilizing radical kindness rooted in spiritual and psychological restoration. Through coaching, teaching, and storytelling, she helps individuals and communities move from survival into embodied wholeness. Her approach blends evidence-based methods, faith-anchored insight, and leadership development for lasting impact.

She holds an M.A. from Gordon-Conwell Theological Seminary that includes a Leadership focus, a B.A. in Journalism from the University of Kansas, and has completed an advanced, year-long program in Evidence-Based Coaching at Fielding University. At the time of this writing, she is at Adler University, has passed her doctoral exams, and is completing the final stretch of her dissertation research.

Melissa is a contributing author to the bestseller *The Rise of Her* and to *Letters to Her*, collaborative works exploring the strength, resilience, and voice of women. She is the solo author of *Whom He Raised*, a memoir and devotional narrative chronicling her personal resurrection story through death to calling to witness, and is developing an upcoming book and workbook centered on Radical Kindness as a Catalyst to the Integrative Transformation Blueprint™.

She is the co-host of the upcoming TV series Mind Shifts and the co-author of the book of the same name, to be released next year.

Melissa has been married to her husband, Darin, for over thirty years, and together they have four daughters. She considers her family life among the most sacred and formative callings of her life.

Her life and leadership have been shaped by decades of navigating physical injury, emotional recovery, spiritual formation, and cultural change. With humility and grit, she carries forward a message of hope: that what once threatened to bury you can become the very ground from which you rise.

Melissa believes in the God who restores, the power of radical forgiveness, fierce love, bold kindness, and the strength of a voice reclaimed.